LAYING CLAIM TO THE MEMORY OF MAY

HAWAI'I STUDIES ON KOREA

WAYNE PATTERSON, *The Ilse: First-Generation Korean Immigrants, 1903–1973* (2000)

LINDA S. LEWIS, *Laying Claim to the Memory of May: A Look Back at the 1980 Kwangju Uprising* (2002)

MICHAEL FINCH, *Min Yŏng-hwan: A Political Biography* (2002)

MICHAEL J. SETH, *Education Fever: Society, Politics, and the Pursuit of Schooling in South Korea* (2002)

HAWAI'I STUDIES ON KOREA

Laying Claim to the Memory of May

A Look Back at the 1980 Kwangju Uprising

LINDA S. LEWIS

University of Hawai'i Press, Honolulu
and
Center for Korean Studies, University of Hawai'i

Library of Congress Cataloging-in-Publication Data

Lewis, Linda Sue.
  Laying claim to the memory of May : a look back at the 1980 Kwangju
uprising / Linda S. Lewis.
    p. cm. — (Hawai'i studies on Korea)
  Includes bibliographical references and index.
  ISBN 0-8248-2479-2 (cloth : alk. paper) — ISBN 0-8248-2543-8 (pbk. : alk.
paper)
    1. Kwangju Uprising, Kwangju-si, Korea, 1980. 2. Korea (South)—Politics
and government—1960–1988. I. Title. II. Series.

DS922.445 .L48 2002
951.904'3—dc21   2001052257

 The Center for Korean Studies was established in 1972 to coordi-
nate and develop resources for the study of Korea at the University
of Hawai'i. Reflecting the diversity of the academic disciplines represented by affiliated members of the university faculty, the
Center seeks especially to promote interdisciplinary and intercultural studies.
Hawai'i Studies on Korea, published jointly by the Center and the University of
Hawai'i Press, offers a forum for research in the social sciences and humanities
pertaining to Korea and its people.

This book is for Cho Kyŏng-suk, Byun Juna,
and Lee Jae-eui, whose compassion
has informed my work.

Contents

Contents

Acknowledgments

MANY OF MY DEBTS OF GRATITUDE in writing this book stretch back twenty years, to the Kwangju Uprising itself. First and foremost, I am grateful to the family of the late Im Ch'ung-nak, who sheltered me in 1980 and who has kindly allowed me to publish parts of my field journal. I have also benefited over the years, in Kwangju, from the kindness and enduring friendship of Judge Chŏn Do-yŏng and Professor Ryang Kae-nam. Although neither has ever agreed with my politics, each has helped me in ways too numerous to recount; I wish to thank them both. Finally, I would like to acknowledge the long-term support of my fellow Koreanists Mark Peterson and Beverly Nelson, whose ties to Kwangju predate my own and with whom I have been able to share, over two decades, an ongoing scholarly and personal interest in 5.18.

During 1995 and 1996, when I conducted most of the research for this book, I found a warm and supportive second home in Seoul at Sogang University. I am particularly appreciative of the friendship and help of Father Basil Price. In addition, I wish to thank the late Father Felix M. Villarreal for his invaluable computer assistance, Hwang Ji-ha and Choe Jeong-sun of the Sogang University Korean Language Education and Research Institute for facilitating the improvement of my language skills, and Professor Sonn Ho-ch'ŏl for our many enlightening discussions about Korean politics. At the time I was serving as the director of the Council on International Educational Exchange

Study Center at Sogang, and I was fortunate in having a sympathetic employer in Ms. Jerry Thompson.

Obviously I could not have completed this book without the kind help of many people in Kwangju, both inside and out of the 5.18 movement. In particular, I would like to thank Byun Juna, Lee Jae-eui, Eugene Suh, Kim Il-hong, and Pak Yŏng-sun. I have also benefited from the research assistance of Kim Ch'ang-ho and Pak Hyŏn-ju of Sogang University and Jae Yoon of Dartmouth College, who helped me read and translate materials.

I have learned that it is necessary, in writing a book, to have friends and colleagues who are willing to read, discuss, and in general support one's efforts. I am grateful for the comments of my colleagues at Wittenberg University—James Huffman, Kent Dixon, Susannah Mintz, and members of the Faculty Works in Progress group—who have read drafts of parts of this book. I have also appreciated the help of Ned Shultz, Mark Peterson, Nancy Ablemann, and one anonymous reader in improving the manuscript. This book is better for my discussions with Roger Janelli, Dawnhee Yim, Fred Carriere, Sallie Yea, and Jeff Wasserstrom and for the emotional boosts I have received from Susannah Mintz, Greg Fraser, and Carol Young, who always asked how the book was coming.

Bits and pieces of this manuscript have been presented over the past five years at colloquia and lectures at Wittenberg University, Dartmouth College, Cornell University, the Association for Asian Studies annual meetings, and in Korea at meetings sponsored by the Royal Asiatic Society, the 5.18 Injured People's Association, and Kwangju Citizens' Solidarity. In addition, I have presented my research at a conference on "Korea after Twenty Years," sponsored by UCLA and USC, and at a workshop on "Civil Society in South Korea" at Columbia University. I appreciate the comments and support I received on those occasions.

Anthropological field research is inevitably a lonely endeavor, and most of my many journeys to Kwangju over the years have been made, literally and/or figuratively, by myself; thus I am particularly grateful to Beverly Nelson and Tobias Smith for the times they came along.

I wish to thank the editorial board of the Hawai'i Studies on Korea series for considering my book and Ned Shultz for suggesting I submit it there. At the University of Hawai'i Press, I am grateful to Patricia

Crosby and Ann Ludeman for their careful management of my manuscript and Bojana Ristich for her scrupulous copyediting.

Finally, I wish to thank my husband, Stephen Smith, who kept me well fed and taught more than his share of summer school courses so I would have the chance to write, and my son, Tobias Smith, veteran of four Uprising anniversary trips to Kwangju, who took pictures for this book.

Research for this book was funded initially (and inadvertently) by a Fulbright doctoral dissertation grant and a Hannum–Werner Travel Fellowship from Mount Holyoke College, both in 1979–1980. More recently, I have appreciated the support of a research travel grant from the Northeast Asia Council of the Association for Asian Studies and two Faculty Research Fund Board grants from Wittenberg University. My travel to Korea in May 2000 was funded by the 5.18 Memorial Foundation.

Part III includes significantly reworked and expanded versions of my articles "Commemorating Kwangju: The 5.18 Movement and Civil Society at the Millennium," in *Korean Society: Civil Society, Democracy, and the State,* ed. Charles Armstrong (forthcoming, Routledge Press), and "The Revictimization of the Direct Victims," in *The Kwangju Uprising after Twenty Years: The Unhealed Wounds of the Victims,* ed. Juna Byun and Linda S. Lewis (Seoul: Dahae Press, 2000). Sections of Part II were originally published as "The 'Kwangju Incident' Observed: An Anthropological Perspective on Civil Uprisings," in *The Kwangju Uprising: Shadows over the Regime in South Korea,* ed. Donald N. Clark (Boulder: Westview Press, 1988).

Note on Transliteration
and Translation

I EMPLOY THE MCCUNE–REISCHAUER SYSTEM of romanization for Korean except for words or names that have a divergent orthography. Korean names are transliterated in the standard fashion: last names first. Translations, unless otherwise indicated, are mine.

Introduction

ON MAY 17, 1995, I SAT on a raised dais at the front of a conference room on the twelfth floor of a new building in downtown Kwangju. Kwangju—at over one million inhabitants, South Korea's fifth largest city but still a regional backwater in comparison with other areas—is the capital of South Chŏlla Province in the extreme southwestern part of the country. I had made the 150-mile trip from Seoul in four hours by train, although in the future I would come to prefer the more convenient fifty-minute commute by air. The building loomed over Kŭmnamno, the city's main thoroughfare, and windows on that side offered magnificent views of Mt. Mudŭng and, below, the street and the central plaza area around the Provincial Office Building; unfortunately, our conference room was at the back, and there was nothing to look at but the audience, which by late afternoon had dwindled to under fifty people. I was there as a participant in an international symposium, "Inhuman Acts and Their Resolution" ("Panillyun Haengwi wa Ch'ŏngsan"), sponsored by the group Kwangju Citizens' Solidarity as its part in the fifteenth anniversary celebration of the Kwangju Uprising.

The Kwangju Uprising (or "5.18," after the date it began) was a popular revolt against the South Korean government that lasted for ten days in May 1980. What began as a peaceful demonstration against the reimposition of military rule turned into a bloody citizens' uprising when the people of Kwangju, outraged by the brutality of government troops sent in to suppress dissent, pushed the soldiers to the edge of town and proclaimed a "Free Kwangju" (haebang Kwangju). The military eventually retook the city with tanks and tear gas but not without great cost in human lives and government credibility.

In retrospect, the Kwangju Uprising stands as one of the most important political events in late twentieth-century Korean history, a powerful symbol of popular opposition to thirty years of repressive military rule and a milestone in South Korea's long journey to democratic reform. Nonetheless, 5.18 also remains, at the millennium, a contested event, the subject still of controversy, confusion, international debate, and competing claims.

I had been asked to join the 1995 symposium because I had witnessed the 1980 uprising and had written about it before. In 1979–1980 I had been in Korea for thirteen months, doing research for my doctoral dissertation. My project concerned the role of judges as mediators in civil disputes, and I had chosen the district court in Kwangju as my research site. Ironically, I first visited Kwangju (to arrange housing) just days after the October 26, 1979, assassination of President Park Chung Hee—retrospectively the first in a chain of events leading to the May uprising.

Actually, my ties to the Chŏlla region predated my 1980 stay in Kwangju. Although most of my seven years of living and working in South Korea have not been spent in the southwest, my first experiences were there. In 1970 as a Peace Corps Volunteer, I was assigned to the agricultural extension office (nongjŏng chidoso) in a small farming village near Kunsan in North Chŏlla Province. I felt comfortable with Chŏlla regional attitudes and liked living in that part of the country enough that I decided to return there for my fieldwork almost a decade later.

While from the mid-1960s the military regime of Park Chung Hee (1961–1979) brought remarkable economic prosperity to South Korea, the benefits of rapid industrial development were unevenly distributed. Where I lived in the early 1970s, the roads were unpaved and the buses crowded, the electricity was erratic, and the nearest bath was public and an hour away. The effects of the central government's pattern of discrimination against the southwest region were visible even then—even I could see that the new superhighway extending south from Seoul stopped at the provincial border—and

The author with Kim Dae Jung and his wife, Lee Hee-ho, at their home in Seoul (February 1985).

while for much of the rest of the nation the rewards of Korea's emergent "economic miracle" outweighed the burdens of authoritarian rule, in the Chŏlla provinces, oppositional sentiment flourished. The farmers with whom I worked were openly critical of the Park regime and supported native son candidate Kim Dae Jung in the 1971 presidential election. When I went back to live in the area in 1979, I found that regional feelings and antagonisms had only intensified.

In the years after I finished my research in Kwangju, I revisited the city several times—including in 1985, when I traveled to Korea with a delegation accompanying Kim Dae Jung home from exile, and again in 1987, when I was there to observe the presidential elections; however, I never had the opportunity to go back for the anniversary events in May. But in 1995 I found myself in Korea once again, this time working in Seoul, and when I was invited to participate in the symposium, I welcomed the chance to return to Kwangju. A colleague at Sogang University, a political science professor, had recommended me for the event; to me, he confided that the sponsoring organization was one of several new groups in the city working to "resolve" the

"5.18 problem"—in this instance by placing the Kwangju Uprising in the context of larger international human rights issues.

I had arrived in Kwangju that morning and had noted with interest and curiosity the many anniversary banners and posters with slogans around the streets; I planned to stay through the next day, although I was not sure exactly what to expect, and now I was anxious for the panel to be done. As I sat listening to the final speech by a representative of the Argentine organization Mothers for the May Plaza Victims (and idly contemplating the fact that I seemed to understand the original Spanish version better than the Korean translation), I heard noise coming from the street below. The sounds of percussion instruments, the cymbals and drums of a traditional farmers' band, bounced off the buildings lining Kŭmnamno and reached the closed auditorium. I watched in frustration as the little group that had come with me from Seoul—my husband, son, and two American college students—quietly eased out of their places at the back of the room to go see what was happening below; it was another thirty minutes before the conference wound down and I could join them at the windows to watch the "Uprising Eve" parade unfolding beneath us.

This book is the result of what I observed on the streets of Kwangju that day and the next. Looking down and back, for block after block, I saw hundreds of citizens and students marching down Kŭmnamno toward the sound stage set up by the plaza fountain. Carrying funeralesque banners, pictures of the dead wrapped with black ribbon, a giant Korean flag, with floats and accompanied by costumed dancers and musicians, they came, reenacting in song and dance the Kwangju People's Uprising story. The parade depicted now famous scenes from May 1980—the local narrative brought to life, stretching out on the street below, familiar episodes retold, memorialized, and celebrated. Later that evening the street would be crammed with people watching the open air Uprising Eve program (Chŏnyaje); afterward, students milled about, singing and dancing around bonfires until midnight. We walked around enthralled. Never had I imagined May in Kwangju would be like this, and I knew right then I wanted to study the 5.18 memorialization process.

In 1995 the relatively quiet fifteenth anniversary commemoration was more like a civic festival than the protest demonstration I had envisioned. In fact, that year it extended for ten days, from May

16 through May 26. In addition to the main events—the Eve Fest on May 17 and the memorial service at the cemetery on May 18—the program also included "Keep the Spirit Alive" and "Prosecute the Murderers" rallies; "Holy Sites Pilgrimage," "Anti-American," and "Democratic Drivers'" days; an international symposium and an academic workshop; a political cartoon display, video showings, performances of a psychodrama, and a *kŭt* (shaman ritual); and Protestant, Catholic, and Chŏndokyŏ religious services. Citizens were asked to take part by burning incense and piling up stones at the cemetery and by mailing preprinted postcards to President Kim Young Sam urging legal action against those responsible for the May massacre.

My experiences in May 1995 turned into four years of research on the 5.18 movement in Kwangju; that work is the basis for Part III in this book. In retrospect, the early 1990s were a turning point in South Korean society. Little did I know as I first watched the celebrations in 1995 that events that year sat on a fault line in Korean political discourse and that my time spent observing the anniversary festivities in Kwangju would span the transition into the post-*minjung* ("people's") era. By the time I finished my research, the class-based political *minjung* movement dominant in the 1970s and 1980s had all but disappeared, to be replaced by the "citizens' groups" of an emergent civil society. The militant, oppositional tone that made the fifteenth anniversary events seem like a kind of political Mardi Gras was banished; by 2000, the increasing commodification of the Kwangju Uprising was underscored by the appearance of a cute little cartoon May 18 mascot, Nuxee, whose smiling visage adorned key chains, T-shirts, and postcards available for purchase by visiting schoolchildren in the 5.18 Democratization Cemetery gift shop. Part III concerns the narratives and practices of commemoration in the 1990s, including the changing signification of the Kwangju Uprising in the context of a newly democratic state.

I found, however, as my research progressed that the boundaries of my project were not so easily drawn. In the late 1980s and early 1990s, when it became possible to publicly discuss the Kwangju Uprising, the Korean-language literature on the subject expanded. By 1995, there were volumes of testimony, memoirs, collections of official documents, and scholarly articles. By 1999, the Kwangju City 5.18 History Committee (5.18 Saryo P'yŏnch'an Wiwŏnhoe) alone had published a fifteen-volume collection of May 18 related materials (*5.18 Kwangju*

minjuhwa undong charyo ch'ongsŏ). Part of my research involved this
vast literature, and I was fascinated by the possibility that every minute
of those days in May was now accounted for. I could look through the
materials, compare the information with my own journal notes and
personal recollections from 1980, and fill in the picture for myself.

I found I also could use the Kwangju Uprising literature to cross-
check people I was encountering during my research on the 5.18
movement in the mid-1990s. Thus before going to Kwangju to inter-
view the chairman of the Injured People's Association, for example, I
could look up his testimony and read his own account of his involvement in the Uprising. I could find out how old he was, how and where
he had been injured, and even what had happened to him during
many of the ensuing years. I found myself moving between 1980 and
the present, in the process learning as much about May 1980 as about
May 1995. I soon realized that in writing about Kwangju in the late
1990s, I would have to begin with the Kwangju Uprising itself.

As I began working on my own Uprising narrative (Part I of this
book), recourse to my field notes and journal entries for May 1980
kept me grounded in the reality of the event itself and in what it felt
like to be in Kwangju at that time. My daily fieldwork journal provided one kind of truth, a reminder of what was and was not known
during those frightening, exhilarating days, as well as what has been
forgotten. My initial impulse in writing Part I was to weave my journal entries into the text, cutting and pasting my observations from
1980 into a well-integrated, seamless 1990s reconstruction of the Uprising. At the very least, I hoped to smooth out the rough edges in my
original field notes—rough edges not just in terms of language and
style, but also of perception, judgment, and subjectivity. At the same
time I did not want simply to rewrite the past with the altered vision
of hindsight; instead, I wished to preserve as much as possible the
voices of a specific time and to engage the reader in the reflexive process of remembering Kwangju over two decades. For this reason, in
the end I chose not to paraphrase my field notes or blend quotations
from my journal into the text; rather, in Parts I and II for the most
part I have included—bad grammar, misspelling, rash statements,
and all—minimally edited sections of my notes and earlier articles.

Thus this became a book with three distinct parts, three narrative positions, and three different ethnographic presents. Part I is a

narrative account of the Kwangju Uprising itself but rooted in the "present" of 1980, through the use of my field notes from that spring and summer. Part II is about the 1980s (specifically 1986, before the end of the Fifth Republic) and recalls the interpretations given 5.18 in a time when it was not possible to speak or write or think freely about May 1980. For this section, I have used materials I wrote in the 1980s. Finally, Part III is about commemorating Kwangju in the late 1990s and is based upon research conducted primarily in Korea between 1995 and 2000.

PART I

Kwangju, 1980

A Narrative Account

5.18 Begins

Violence and Confusion on the City's Streets

May 18

THE 1980 KWANGJU UPRISING BEGAN on Sunday, May 18, when a relatively small group of about two hundred college students, in defiance of a military ban on political activities, marched to the Provincial Office Building in the heart of downtown Kwangju and held a peaceful demonstration. Chanting "End martial law!," "Free Kim Dae Jung!," and "Down with Chun Doo Hwan" (head of the ruling military junta) (Hwang Sŏh Yŏng 1985:37), the by now five hundred demonstrators were at first met by riot police with tear gas who attempted to disperse the crowds. But in the early afternoon military troops began arriving in the city. By 3 P.M. the regular police had been replaced on the main thoroughfares by armed soldiers, particularly the Special Warfare Command (SWC) airborne troops of the Seventh Brigade (Thirty-third and Thirty-fifth Battalions), and the demonstrations quickly turned bloody.

The "black beret" Special Forces were specially trained for hand-to-hand combat behind the lines in North Korea and were never intended for deployment against their own friendly civilian demonstrators.[1] To the shock and horror of onlookers, the paratroopers aggressively attacked protestors and bystanders alike, chasing, grabbing, beating, and arresting anyone in sight. In response, angry citizens joined in, throwing rocks, demolishing police substations, and fighting the soldiers at several locations around the central city. The

3

few thousand protestors were eventually overwhelmed and forced to scatter, however, as the provincial Martial Law Command imposed a 9 P.M. curfew in Kwangju.

I had gone to Seoul the week before, on May 15, to give a lecture and had watched the massive protests there. Tens of thousands of students demanding the repeal of martial law and the resignation of Chun Doo Hwan had been holding increasingly violent demonstrations in the capital and in major cities throughout the nation (including Kwangju).[2] The largest yet were planned for Friday, May 16, but student leaders, suspecting further violent protests would provide the excuse the military was looking for to take control, called them off, and Seoul was suddenly quiet. Then on Saturday night (May 17) the government announced a crackdown: martial law was extended, political activity banned, and opposition social and political leaders were detained.[3] One of the politicians arrested that day in Seoul was Kim Dae Jung, a native of Mokp'o (near Kwangju) and the Chŏlla provinces' "favorite son." Kim Dae Jung later would stand trial and be sentenced to death for his alleged part in "masterminding" the Kwangju Uprising.[4]

I heard the news about the government's repressive actions on the morning of Sunday, May 18, as I was on my way to the Seoul Express Bus Terminal. The expansion of military control seemed certain to provoke an explosive reaction from students, most likely another round of violent street fighting. Boarding a bus for the five-hour ride back to Kwangju, I felt some regret at leaving the center of political activity. I did not expect that the only demonstrations that day would be in Kwangju, nor could I have anticipated that in the ten days that followed Seoul and other cities would remain quiet as the events in Kwangju failed to trigger a nationwide response.

The successful isolation of Kwangju and the surrounding Honam region in its rebellion was at the time a source of dismay, disbelief, and bewilderment to those who lived there, and it remains a point of some speculation into the present.[5] In early May 1980 the entire country seemed poised on the brink of insurrection—why did Kwangju's citizens stand alone? Certainly the military government's blackout of information on what was happening in Kwangju provides, retrospectively, a partial explanation. Phone lines were cut and the Chŏlla provinces sealed off, and national news media made no mention for days of the violence that was unfolding in the southwest.

Regional prejudice suggests a more complex picture. Kwangju natives remain convinced that the government would have been more cautious in using deadly force against the people of other cities and that their fellow Koreans would have been less willing to tolerate the massacre of innocent citizens elsewhere in the country. "Finding the truth" (*chinsang kyumyŏng*) about 5.18 and making sure that others know what went on has been and continues to be the focus of almost two decades of struggle by Kwangju citizens, as we shall see.

Late 1979 to the spring of 1980 was a time of transition in South Korean political history, a period of both optimism and confusion in the moment between the death of one military dictator—Park Chung Hee was assassinated by the head of his own intelligence agency—and the formal seizure of power by another, Chun Doo Hwan, the following summer. After Park's assassination Prime Minister Choi Kyu-ha had succeeded to the presidency with the anticipation of a return to civilian rule, but the country was still under partial martial law; after

Author with members of family with whom she lived in Kwangju (September 1980).

what has been termed a "coup-like incident" within the military on December 12, 1979, Chun Doo Hwan emerged as the country's new strongman. Even so, in the first months of 1980 there were popular hopes throughout Korea for democratic reforms and the dismantling of the late president's repressive Yusin system.[6]

These hopes were particularly strong in Kwangju, the largest city in the economically depressed Honam region but still something of a tranquil backwater surrounded by striking mountains and rice paddies. In 1980 I was a boarder with a family in Kyerim 3-dong, near the center of town. I had watched people's expectations of democratization dim through the winter and early so-called "Democracy Spring" (*minjuhwa pom*) as the army signaled its intention, beginning with the coup d'état of December 12, to remain in control of the government.

May 19

> *They're killing people down here today—again. Lots died yesterday, too, although I didn't find out about it until today. After all the gas and ruckus in Seoul on Thursday, then nothing on Friday and Saturday, then the announcement of more martial law on Sunday morning—Seoul was quiet. But Kwangju. . . . I got back at suppertime on Sunday [May 18], on a bus one-third full of soldiers. The whole bus station was full of soldiers in fact, and there were lots of extra buses. . . . But it was only today I knew something would happen—the streets looked tense. Started at 11 A.M. for the ACC [American Cultural Center], got as far as the street where they are building the underwalk, and it was blocked by soldiers—not riot police, special forces soldiers. People were going through and crowds were gathering, but I decided not to venture forth. I went home, and Mother came panting in shortly after, semi-hysterical. On the main drag [Kŭmnamno] she had seen a student bayoneted, front to back, and thrown on a police van. . . . After Mother talked about what she had seen, Tong-nip said there had been riots the day before, and reports had as high as 30 killed (field journal, May 19, 1980).*

After my initial hesitation on Monday morning, May 19—the second day of the Kwangju Uprising—I did go out again, to the courthouse. Only this time, when in the late afternoon I returned to my home in a residential section about a ten-minute walk from the Provincial Office

Building, I went by way of back streets and alleys, avoiding the main thoroughfares, which were blocked off at the intersections by lines of soldiers. The streets were virtually empty of traffic. Most of the shops were already shuttered, and the rest were quickly being closed. In contrast, many of the side streets were jammed from where they joined the main roads, filled with angry citizens milling about, talking in groups, tense, frightened, and upset. The small commercial street nearest my home was also full of people. I was told it had been the scene not ten minutes before of a pitched battle between soldiers and citizens. The soldiers had driven my neighbors back up the street and into the alleys.

The street fighting had been continuing on May 19 since the morning, when by 10 A.M. three to four thousand demonstrators had gathered on Kŭmnamno, and many ordinary citizens going about their business downtown (like the mother in my household) witnessed random acts of brutality and were inadvertently caught up in the escalating violence. Paratroopers of the Eleventh Brigade occupied strategic locations in the center of the city; protestors threw rocks and Molotov cocktails, blew up oil drums, and erected barricades with concrete flower boxes, public telephone booths, street signs, and iron traffic barriers (Hwang Sŏk Yŏng 1985:62–64). Elementary schools closed, and middle and high school students started demonstrating on their campuses. In the afternoon the fighting intensified. The Munhwa Broadcasting Corporation (MBC) building was set on fire, as were several police substations.[7] The military began using armored vehicles to suppress the demonstrations, and helicopters flew overhead announcing, "Citizens, please go home. We cannot guarantee your life if you remain on the streets. Citizens, be assured that the martial law forces are doing their best to restore order in the city" (Hwang Sŏk Yŏng 1985:74).

Lunching with a group of judges, I was puzzled that no one was talking much about the demonstrations going on a short taxi ride away. Finally, I discovered my friends were not being reticent or indifferent; they simply did not have much information (only rumors). Townspeople, especially young males, were afraid to go out. I learned this when some young male clerks (in their early twenties) urged me to go downtown, explaining that the judges could not go out because as public servants if they were to be seen anywhere near a demonstration, they would get in trouble. And the clerks themselves, because of their

Grave site of Kim Kyŏng-ch'ŏl, first Kwangju Uprising victim, in 5.18 Cemetery.

youth, would be mistaken for college students and would risk being grabbed and beaten by the soldiers. But you (they told me) are a foreign woman and as such are the only one here who can safely walk about.

The fear these young men felt was, as it turned out, well founded—just as the experience of the *ajumŏni* (matron) in my household that morning on the downtown streets was not an isolated event. Now, many years later, every minute of the ten days of the 5.18 Kwangju People's Uprising is well documented. It is possible to read eyewitness accounts, personal testimony, and collections of records that provide compelling evidence of the horrible events going on in the city and the terror, confusion, and anger that Kwangju citizens felt, especially on May 18 and 19. There is, for example, the story of the first victim, who died on May 18. His name was Kim Kyŏng-ch'ŏl, and he was a twenty-seven-year-old shoe salesman. In the monumental 5.18 Democratization Cemetery, completed in 1997, the victims have been reinterred in order of their deaths. Kim Kyŏng-ch'ŏl's grave is the first one visitors encounter, immediately to the left after coming up the stairs under the memorial tower. The following is what the 5.18

Kwangju People's Uprising Bereaved Families' Association (5.18 Kwangju
Minjung Hangjaeng Yujokhoe) memorial book tells of his death:

> It was Kim Kyŏng-ch'ŏl, deaf and mute since taking the wrong medi-
> cine as a child, who was the first victim of the paratroopers during the
> Kwangju Massacre. Mr. Kim, an administrative officer of the Kwangju
> Committee of the Deaf and Mute, had gone to the bus terminal on the
> morning of 5.18 to see off his brother-in-law, who had come from
> Seoul. On his way back home, he was attacked on Kŭmnamno, at the
> underground shopping mall construction site, by paratroopers who
> beat him to death. It was when the paratroopers first came into the city.
>
> Many people witnessed the paratroopers beating Mr. Kim, who,
> with two hands folded, was begging for his life. According to them, he
> was beaten because he could not understand the paratroopers' words
> and could not respond to their directions and commands and could
> not explain his own situation, so he was beaten to death. It could not
> but be a sorrowful sight. In truth, Kim Kyŏng-ch'ŏl, a man unable to
> speak or hear, could not even cry out one word of a slogan—'With-
> draw martial law!' or 'Down with Chun Doo Hwan!' For what reason
> did he need to be butchered by the paratroopers sent into Kwangju?
> According to the citizens who witnessed this sad scene, the paratroop-
> ers thought that it was a lie that he could not speak, and so they beat
> him into submission, and he did not answer, so they kicked him with
> their boots, and they thought he was just playing with them, pretend-
> ing to be a deaf-mute, so they stomped on him.
>
> According to the autopsy reports, Kim suffered cuts and bruises on
> his head, face, arms, legs, and hips and a broken neck (BFA 1989: 235).

In the late afternoon on May 19 (as I was walking home), Kim
Kyŏng-ch'ŏl's mute young wife canvassed the hospitals and his mother
went out to the makeshift jail at Sangmudae (the military base at the edge
of town) looking for information about him (KMHRI 1990:1232–1233).

There are many eyewitness accounts of the viciousness of the paratroopers on May 18 and 19 and stories of the response of onlookers. Lee
Jae-eui describes running from soldiers several times, once hiding in a
cabinet and another time escaping detection by grabbing a hammer at
a construction site and blending in with the men working there. He also
tells of looking down from the roof of the suburban bus terminal on the

afternoon of May 18; below, paratroopers had rounded up about fifteen students who were kneeling down, heads to the ground. Suddenly, a student in the back stood up, hollering, "Feet—save me!," and made a dash for safety in a nearby market area. People on the roof started cheering, and the paratroopers began beating the other students. Onlookers responded by hurling things off the roof at the soldiers, and some rushed down below to pelt them with paving stones (KMHRI 1990:328).

Foreign residents too were inadvertent witnesses. The Korea Baptist Convention and the Florida Convention were having an evangelistic crusade. The American participants were staying at the Kwangju Tourist Hotel on Kŭmnamno, and they and their local host, Arnold Peterson (a Baptist missionary), observed repeated incidents of military brutality as they tried to make their way to and from their lodgings in the center of town. At 5:30 P.M. they were walking on Kŭmnamno behind a neatly dressed young man when he was suddenly confronted by three paratroopers who began to question him. As Peterson and his colleagues looked on,

> They immediately began to hit the young man about the ribs, back, and shoulders with their batons, and forced him to his knees. They questioned him, implying that he was involved in the demonstrations. The young man protested that he was merely on his way home, but his words fell on deaf ears. He protested that he had been doing nothing and begged to be allowed to leave. They continued to beat him, kick him in the groin, and lunged at him with a bayonet. The bayonet stopped only inches from his throat (A. Peterson 1995:191–192).

The next day the horrified Floridians told of seeing hundreds of students on the streets being beaten with clubs, kicked, punched with rifle butts, and, stripped to their underwear, with hands tied behind their backs, being either marched off down the street or loaded onto trucks and carted away (A. Peterson 1995:196–197).

An American Peace Corps Volunteer, Tim Warnberg, was downtown at about 3 P.M. on May 18 when the paratroopers first began charging at crowds:

> We ran with the panicked crowd and I ended up in a small store along with about fifteen other people, including one other PCV. A soldier

came into the store and proceeded to club everyone over the head with his truncheon until he came to the other volunteer and me. He stopped startled, hesitated a moment, then ran out. We went out into the side street and found that the troops had retreated to the main street, leaving behind wounded people everywhere. . . . Two volunteers and I picked up a delivery boy for a Chinese restaurant who had been knocked off his bike with a blow to his head. We brought him to a clinic and managed to convince the reluctant doctor to open his door. He said he feared retaliation from the military. Other wounded people filled the streets and tried to push their way in, but he only let about ten people in before he locked the door again. People banged on the door cursing and screaming (Warnberg 1988:39).

The next day, Warnberg reports trying to help a Korean doctor carry wounded citizens off the streets. The soldiers were forcing the injured to sit in the middle of the road. Warnberg and the doctor were able to carry some of the worst cases to a clinic before the soldiers refused to let them back through the lines. "The remaining thirty or so injured were forced to run a gauntlet to the back of a military truck and climb in on their own power" (Warnberg 1988:40).

At my own house on May 19 (when I finally reached it), there were three strange high school girls. No one in the family knew them, but they could not travel around the city that evening to return to their own homes, so they just stayed with us until morning. Members of my household were in turmoil. Everyone was concerned about Father getting home from his job as an elementary school principal in the countryside. Indeed, there were large demonstrations going on around the suburban bus terminal through which he had to pass. My *ajumŏni*, who had witnessed the bayoneting on Kŭmnamno that morning, now heard that a grade school child, along with other citizens, had been killed nearby in the recent street fighting. Her daughter, Yun-ok, the youngest of four children and a third-year high school student, was worried that she and her classmates in Kwangju would fall behind the rest of the country in studying for their college entrance exams. And Tong-nip, a junior at Chŏnnam University, had heard a lot of rumors, among them that the head of the student body at his school had been killed and that soldiers were making house-to-house searches looking for students.

His mother of course would not let Tong-nip near the front gate, although she herself wanted to go out and join the protestors. Indeed, Tong-nip, like many other young people in Kwangju, remained confined to the house for the entire period of the civil unrest. Initially, when young people were the principal targets of the violence, students stayed inside out of concern for their safety; many of them then remained in hiding, even during the least dangerous phases of the rebellion, for fear they would later be singled out as culpable. Although 5.18 has been characterized as a student uprising, college students in fact were just the catalysts, the first participants. It was only a relatively small group of them who were active, and armed, throughout the entire event. Students comprised just 19.5 percent of the official victims and were only a slight majority (fifteen of twenty-eight) of those killed on the last day (May 27), when the army retook the Provincial Office Building (BFA 1989:335–336). Like tens of thousands of others around the country, Tong-nip had been demonstrating the previous week as part of an ongoing national pattern of protests against the imposition of martial law. But as his mother explained to me on May 14, as she anxiously awaited his return home from a demonstration, "I agree with him that the government is bad, but I urge him not to demonstrate because I worry about him. He could get hurt, or jailed, or thrown out of school. I have a friend whose daughter has been out of school for three years, and was just reinstated. She can't get married until she finishes school, but how can she finish school? And her father is a policeman" (field journal). Even by May 19, students had been largely replaced on Kwangju's streets by ordinary citizens, particularly young working-class men, as worried parents kept their children indoors or sent them to the countryside to stay with relatives.[8]

That evening I called the Fulbright director, Mark Peterson, who had taken me to the bus terminal in Seoul just the day before, to reassure him that I was safe; he had heard nothing about the violence in Kwangju. The military had imposed a blackout on news about what was happening down south, presumably to prevent the riots from spreading to other parts of the country. Although word spread quickly through phone calls such as my own,[9] and in the next few days through the reports of both domestic and foreign journalists,[10] the lack of official acknowledgment of the disturbance coupled with the incredible nature of the rumors and stories that did circulate meant that the brutality in Kwangju provoked no nationwide popular response. I noted on May 19 that "the worst thing for people here is that the rest of the country doesn't know what is going on. . . . Everyone is stunned—heartsick. . . . I can't say I feel frightened, certainly not for my personal safety. . . . But it is really horrible, and people can't believe it is happening, and can't imagine why" (field journal).

Why, indeed? Local explanations in those first days for the apparently random and senseless brutality of the soldiers sent into Kwangju focused on reports that their breath smelled of alcohol, that they were on some sort of drugs, that they had been denied food, and that they all spoke in a Kyŏngsang Province dialect.[11] This was, people speculated, part of a conspiracy against the Honam region; the government was trying to kill all the young men in the Chŏlla provinces.

The apparent outlandishness of the hearsay, suppositions, and allegations about the paratroopers that flew about in those first days mirrored the incomprehensibility of what people saw taking place around them. Even to those who experienced it, the savagery was unbelievable. And if the vision of a soldier bayoneting a student on Kŭmnamno was beyond the imagination of my *ajumŏni*, who witnessed it with her own eyes, how could such a story be credible to her fellow countrymen in Seoul—or, for that matter, be a realistic, even probable, scenario in the minds of the chronically out-of-touch diplomats in the U.S. Embassy? The "why" of the Kwangju massacre still remains (as we shall see), as does the skepticism and denial of many people, for whom 5.18 has always been beyond belief.

The "Righteous" Rebellion

Citizens Fight Back

May 20

The battle of Kwangju, Day 3, closes to the sound of automatic weapons. That followed (at 11 P.M.) the [tear] gassing of the city at 10. We went out—saw fires, then couldn't breathe. Within 15 minutes the whole neighborhood was silent. At 8 P.M. we all went out—shouts from the city. . . . The whole city was full, jammed. Special forces had been replaced by regular soldiers. TV stations were off the air (burned?). We thought the revolution had come. Nervous knots of people out everywhere. People with children. Pounding footsteps on back alleys. . . . This followed a harrowing day. Rain in the morning, which put a damper on things (field journal, May 20, 1980).

WHILE DEMONSTRATIONS WERE SLOW to start on Tuesday, May 20, by night time the whole central part of town was literally as well as figuratively inflamed. MBC, the Kwangju Tax Office, the Provincial Office Building car depot, and sixteen police substations were burned down, and the Korea Broadcasting System (KBS) and the Labor Supervision Office had been set on fire; there were vehicles in flames all over town. Insurgents controlled all but the Kwangju train station and the Provincial Office Building, and by 4:00 A.M. (May 21) the station had been taken as well (Hwang Sŏk Yŏng 1985:79–105). That night, soldiers began shooting M-16s into the crowds of demonstrators at Chŏnnam University (*New York Times*, May 22, 1980). "Provincial City Resembles

14

Armed Camp," proclaimed the *Asian Wall Street Journal* headline; it continued: "Reporters arriving by train Tuesday morning [May 20] found eight truckloads of armed soldiers guarding the station plaza and the wreckage of burned out trucks and cars still smoldering in the streets. Tanks and armored cars block bridges and some main streets, and a park where some of the riots took place is completely sealed off by troops" (May 21, 1980). Indeed, the revolution *had* come; by the afternoon of May 20, 5.18 was a civil uprising, with reportedly one to two hundred thousand of the general citizenry (or up to one quarter of the city's population) engaged in the increasingly fierce resistance.[1]

Initially and as an explanation of what had provoked most of the street fighting in the first days, ordinary people took to the streets as an expression of popular outrage at the brutality of government troops in suppressing the demonstrations. Many people first joined in the uprising in the context of neighborhood fighting, through either witnessing some violent incident themselves or hearing a firsthand account of it. It was difficult, in fact, to totally avoid involvement in those early days because so much street fighting went on. People went out to look and got caught up in it or were in the streets searching for a friend or family member and were swept up in the violence. In addition, by May 20 there was general frustration and anger that there was no coverage in the domestic media of the catastrophe engulfing Kwangju.

Nowadays, May 20 is celebrated in Kwangju as "Minju Kisa ŭi Nal" (Democratic Drivers' Day) in recognition of the decisive role played by taxi drivers at this point in the uprising. At 7 P.M. a convoy of hundreds of honking vehicles (noisy enough to be heard in my courtyard) full of demonstrators, with trucks, express buses, and city buses in the lead, followed by hundreds of taxi cabs, set out from Mudŭng Stadium toward the Provincial Office Building to charge the cordons of soldiers and try to break through their lines. Now famous photos of this climactic *ch'aryang siwi* (vehicle demonstration) show a young man standing atop the first bus, waving a Korean flag, as the procession approaches downtown (Hwang and Kim 1991:38–39). The idea for the vehicle demonstrations came from a small group of cab drivers who, aware of the actions of the soldiers from their trips around the city and also enraged by incidents where taxi drivers assisting the injured and taking passengers to hospitals had been assaulted themselves, decided to organize transportation workers.

Vehicle demonstrations were inspirational but dangerous; martial law troops used tear gas to daze the drivers, then pulled them out
of their cars and beat them. Vehicles went out of control and crashed
on the street. The next day (May 21), participants (drivers and passengers alike) risked being shot. In fact, many of the injured were riding
in trucks and buses when they were wounded, and fully 8.5 percent
(or fourteen) of 5.18 victims are classified as "*unjŏnja*" (drivers)(BFA
1989:335).[2] The memorial record for one of them is as follows:

> Mr. Kim Pong-man, who was a bus driver for the Hyŏndae Transpor-
> tation Company, had been conveying injured people from all around
> the city to hospitals since May 18. But after May 21 he did not get in
> touch with his landlady, whom he was to call to let her know how he
> was while his wife was in Changsŏng because of her mother's death.
> His family members assume it is obvious that he played a leading role
> in the vehicle demonstrations and drove in front of the Provincial
> Office Building on May 21. He was found dead by his friend at the Red
> Cross hospital with a gunshot wound in his back and was laid in state
> at Sangmugwan [the military gymnasium across from the Provincial
> Office Building]. His wife, who returned to Kwangju on May 24,
> rushed straight to Sangmugwan, but his body had already been placed
> in a coffin. At the time her children were three years old and one
> month. After confirming that he was dead, she wailed, venting her re-
> sentment. Nothing could completely rid her of her sorrow short of
> her desire to follow after her dead husband. But her two children were
> too young for her to do that.
>
> In the paratroopers' Kwangju massacre that started on May 18,
> they beat even taxi and bus drivers carrying the wounded to hospitals,
> with riot sticks, and stabbed them with bayonets, saying they were
> told to kill all the "Kwangju bastards." The paratroopers sent into
> Kwangju were ordered only to kill Kwangju citizens, not to take casu-
> alties to hospitals and treat them. Nothing but killing with riot sticks
> and M-16s with bayonets. Mr. Kim Pong-man was a driver caring for
> the injured, and he seems to have been in one of the leading vehicles
> in the May 21 demonstration on Kŭmnamno. What on earth does the
> "right of self-defense" of the paratroopers who killed him have to do
> with explaining the truth about Kwangju?
>
> Whenever she is reminded of the uncertainty of life, Mrs. Kang

Sŏng-sun, who has lost her husband, goes with her two children to Mangwŏl-dong cemetery (BFA 1989:199).

For those who would situate the Kwangju Uprising as an important juncture in the history of the Korean working-class movement or who would interpret 5.18 as a narrative of emergent class struggle, the vehicle demonstrations marked another crucial turning point in the unfolding drama. As the journalist Lee Jae-eui observed in his detailed account of the uprising, "The spontaneously generated strength of the transportation workers and the transformative power of their unified movement showed the potential of the masses. It was a beautiful moment when, of their own accord, the people threw their lives into the forefront of history. The look in their eyes, their solidarity, and their selfless determination were the high point of the May uprising; a tidal wave swept through the whole city from the evening of the 20th until the dawning of the next day" (Hwang Sŏk Yŏng 1985:85).[3]

Lee's hyperbolic phraseology aside, claims of organized labor to the memory of 5.18 are strong, and contingents of union members are a highly visible, often militant, presence at the May commemoration events in Kwangju. In fact, student and labor movement representatives are the only real participants of note from outside the Honam region. In 1997 the inauguration of the newly formed National Democratic Taxi Drivers' Federated Union (Chŏn'guk Minju T'aeksi Nodong Chohap Yŏnmaeng) was held in Kwangju on May 20 in conjunction with the annual Democratic Drivers' Day memorial service and reenactment. The head of the national democratic labor movement spoke, as did the Seventeenth Anniversary Events Committee chairman; Kwangju civic leaders and local transportation union officials shared the lead truck in the vehicle parade downtown to the Provincial Office Building. To the taxi driver from Taegu who stood beside me at the rally in 1997 and spoke of the historical importance of 5.18 to his new union, worker solidarity in this case overrode traditional regional animosities (and the personal discomfort he himself confessed to feeling at being in Kwangju on that day).

In 1980 on May 20, it was possible in the morning and early afternoon (before the fires and violence of the night) to go out via back alleys. Away from the main streets, shops were open, public transportation was running, and there was no sign of soldiers, although there were few people on the streets. I went with no difficulty to the court-house, where several judges I knew were sitting around, anxiously comparing notes. Despondent and often near tears, they expressed their worries and fear about what was happening outside. After an hour or so, I went to the house of a friend nearby, a college art profes-sor who was showing me how to do *maedŭp* (a traditional Korean form of decorative knot tying). Still, we had trouble concentrating on knots, as our conversation kept turning to events downtown. Even my normally apolitical teacher could not stop nervously speculating about what was going on. Finally, I went home, again with no prob-lems, except that crowds were gathering near the main roads and the major intersection was closed off by troops.

In my own household, we all had more rumors and gossip to share. Tension was also mounting over the issue of the failure of the U.S. government to intervene; on May 20 I recorded the following conversation with the father in my family, who knew that I was in fre-quent contact with David Miller, the director of the local ACC and the sole American official in Kwangju:

> FATHER: Miller is a real bastard—he isn't calling Seoul.
> ME: But he is.
> FATHER: No—if he were, the U.S. would do something.

I will discuss the controversy over the U.S. role during 5.18 below; on May 20, the question in Kwangju was quite simply why American sol-diers were not coming to the defense of the city.

To the members of my family, the lack of some overt American action was taken as evidence that the American Embassy in Seoul did not understand what was happening in Kwangju, and this idea came from the apparent conviction (to my friends clearly obvious, to me naive, even fantastic) that the U.S. government would intervene to stop the violence. As a U.S. citizen, in the early days of the uprising I was continually questioned, not with hostility but with dismay and confusion, about the apparent lack of any American response.

As it happened, David Miller was indeed calling Seoul. But in the U.S. Embassy on May 20, the benefit of the doubt remained with the Martial Law Command and Korean government officials. The U.S. government has stated that it first learned of the situation in Kwangju from Miller on the morning of May 19 (when he told of reports that the paratroopers were responsible for numerous casualties and even some deaths) and that the U.S. Embassy's "fragmentary" knowledge of events during May 19 and 20 was based on Miller's information, the limited observations of U.S. Air Force officials at the base outside the city, and reports from foreign journalists (USIS 1989:14–15). However, since the reports from Kwangju "contrasted so greatly with the sullen, repressed, but non-violent atmosphere in Seoul, it was at first difficult for the Embassy to understand their full significance" (USIS 1989:14); in addition, Miller's information was scanty because he was ordered, for security reasons, to remain indoors, and official Korean sources "either denied there was any particular problem in Kwangju or downplayed the seriousness of events there" (USIS 1989:15). The paratroopers were being driven from the city by the time the U.S. government began to take the situation in Kwangju seriously, and then the embassy's concern was more with external security and political stability than with internal abuse of military force.

May 21

Buddha's birthday—a national holiday. Day 4 of the Kwangju insurrection. Things are so tense, I don't want to type. A gorgeous, clear day—warm, even hot. Things began early—as soon as the fog cleared and there was good visibility, the helicopters started overflights and the citizens took to the streets. . . . All phone lines to Seoul—or anywhere—are out. So, apparently, is all access to the city. . . . A festive atmosphere prevails. People on rooftops, sitting on the hilltops, on balconies of apartments. I wish I had a vantage point. Almost everything—especially on the main street—is closed and shuttered. Knots of people sit and talk. The brave make it down to the yakkuk [pharmacy], past women wrapping kim *[dried seaweed] around rice and packing it in boxes to give to students. A notice [from student activists] is tacked up down by the* yakkuk, *on a public phone, giving a plan [of action]: students in from Chŏndae [Chŏnnam National University], high school students from Sansu Naegori [Sansu intersection] to the Toch'ŏng [Provincial Office Building]—everyone else [ordinary citizens] to the Toch'ŏng. It is a promenade down to the rotary [the Kyerim 5 street intersection]—people out with their kids. Much tension. . . . Every so often a truck*

whizzes by, horn honking, flags waving, full of cheering students geared for
battle. People cheer. . . . No soldiers anywhere. But I don't trust them. They
will appear, suddenly, and maybe with guns. . . . The only thing the radio
[The U.S. Armed Forces Korea Network (AFKN), in English, which so far
had not mentioned Kwangju] is saying is, "U.S. citizens, don't go to
Kwangju. More news when the situation is clarified." That means no one
knows what is going on here, exactly (field journal, May 21, 1980).

While Wednesday, May 21, may have begun with a general air of nervous expectation and increasingly militant defiance and bravado and
ended in triumph in the evening with the complete withdrawal of the
soldiers from the center of town, it was also, in retrospect, the blood-
iest single day of the Kwangju Uprising. There were sixty-two official
dead, most (fifty-four) killed by gunshot, the majority (66 percent) in
the vicinity of the Provincial Office Building (BFA 1989:336). While
young men with guns in their hands and grenades hanging from their
jacket pockets rode around in commandeered army trucks (KMHRI
1990:331) and weapons were being distributed at such places as
Kwangju Park (*Asian Wall Street Journal,* May 23, 1980, p. A1) and the
Kyerim police box near my home (KMHRI 1990:330), most of the casualties on May 21 were unarmed citizens, shot down as troops repeatedly fired into crowds of demonstrators gathered downtown and
in front of the Chŏnnam University gate (KCSPRI 1991:287).

The fighting had continued all of the previous night. At 2 A.M.
the Third Brigade had retreated from Kwangju Station to Chŏnnam
University. Long-distance phones lines had been cut and the city
sealed off.[4] At dawn, the KBS television and radio station had been set
on fire. At 9 A.M., insurgents had broken into the Asia Truck Factory
and appropriated fifty-six large trucks (KCSPRI 1991:287). Increasingly violent vehicle demonstrations were forming, and one hundred
thousand demonstrators thronged the main streets.

Just before 10 A.M. three citizens' representatives met with the
provincial governor. They asked for a public apology for the bloodshed, the release of students and citizens who had been detained, and
information about those who had been hospitalized; they also demanded the withdrawal of martial law forces from the city by noon
(May 21). The governor promised to try to get the soldiers withdrawn
and agreed to the other demands. But as the morning wore on, the

governor never appeared to apologize, and the situation remained the same (KMHRI 1990:56). The crowds on Kŭmnamno continued to grow, and leaflets (like the student activists' plan of action I had seen posted up) asked people to gather downtown at 2 P.M. As the martial law soldiers prepared their retreat from the Provincial Office Building, helicopters landed to take away important papers.

Shortly after noon, soldiers in front of the Provincial Office Building began firing. Lee Jae-eui relates how he and some other students were in the Noktu bookstore: "At about 1 P.M. we talked back and forth about what countermeasures we could take, when suddenly we heard a thunk and a rat-a-tat sound. We went out. In the vicinity of the labor office tens of citizens had fallen in an instant. The soldiers had begun to fire indiscriminately in front of them, at the gathered citizens. If they were hit by gunfire, three or four people dragged those who had fallen, and everyone's faces were white with shock. Citizens kept falling. And among them were even students who looked like they were in high school" (cited in KMHRI 1990:330).

Martha Huntley, an American missionary, wrote later that when the soldiers started firing on citizens,

> The bullets, fired from M-16 rifles, were the kind that exploded on contact—a violation of the Geneva Convention. My husband and I were at the Kwangju Christian Hospital the afternoon of May 22 at 3 P.M. when this first happened.[5] In two hours our hospital alone received 99 wounded and 14 dead. Among the wounded were a 9-year-old boy who was shot in the legs. Our first dead was a middle school girl; the second was a commercial high school girl who had donated blood at the hospital 15 minutes earlier and was shot by the troops as she was being returned home in a student vehicle. We received five patients with spinal cord injuries, many of whom will never walk again. One was 13 years old. We had other patients who lost eyes, limbs, and their minds (Huntley 1982:13).

One of those most seriously injured that afternoon was Kim Yong-dae. As he related in testimony in 1988, at the time of 5.18, his wife was pregnant with their second child; in fact, she was almost ready to deliver and was having problems. On May 19 and 20 he heard at the Samyang tire factory where he worked that citizens were being killed, but he did not completely believe the rumors. On May 21, like every day, he went to work. The bus was late, and he heard that the factory was closed and that the night before *simin'gun* (citizens' militia) had come and stolen tires. Just then, a confrontation started at the bus station, and he started to participate. He thought of going to tell his family first, but he felt he would be a coward if he did not join in. He also wanted to see with his own eyes if the rumors were true. So he went to the Provincial Office Building for confirmation. A vehicle demonstration was going on at 9 A.M., and he went to Kŭmnamno five blocks from the Provincial Office Building to see for himself. He saw an armored personnel carrier in the street. He got to the Provincial Office Building at 10 A.M., at which time there was a standoff between the citizens and soldiers. At around noon, about twenty people got on a bus, and the soldiers opened fire. When that happened, citizens ran, and he himself ran toward the YWCA. Again citizens approached the Provincial Office Building, again the soldiers opened fire, and again the citizens ran. He was hit by a shot from an M-16, his spinal cord was cut, and he was paralyzed from the waist down. People took him to the Christian Hospital. His wife was also in the hospital at the time, having a Caesarian section (KMHRI 1990:726–729).

When I met Kim Yong-dae in 1996 at his apartment (where he is confined, in chronic pain, to a water bed), he told me, "Frankly, I really hate to talk about 5.18. My child, who was born then, is now in high school. My kid was born the very next day after I was shot. People today don't understand the story, don't understand why we needed to do that, and how we rose up. Even today thinking about it makes us feel anxious and drives us crazy." He recalled that in 1980, "I wasn't even thirty—and now I am almost fifty. But at that time, I was a little older [than most victims]; victims were mostly in their twenties. Statistics say there were about two thousand victims, all young and unemployed." He recounted that he had even sent his own college-age cousin away to his hometown before the 21st, and "On the 21st most of the students had retreated from the front—they had all been captured or escaped. So it was just innocent citizens attacking the soldiers. We have to focus on the spirit of 5.18. . . . It took a long time for it to be recognized as a citizens' movement."

Pak Yŏng-sun, who with several others started the Injured People's Association (5.18 Minjung Hangjaeng Pusangja Hoe) in 1982, was also hurt on May 21. A student then, he, like Kim Yong-dae, had been just an observer until he joined a vehicle demonstration that morning. He was in the fifth car when the soldiers opened fire. The driver was not wounded so could turn around. Although Pak ducked down, he was still hit, and one in their group was killed (KMHRI 1990:689–691).

Those who died on May 21, as on other days during the uprising, also included some of the most truly innocent of victims. Kim Myŏng-ch'ŏl, a sixty-five-year-old businessman with four grown children, was feeling anxious about his son and so was standing in front of his home waiting for him when a paratrooper approached and began beating him about the head with a riot stick. His youngest son searched the city for two days until, randomly opening coffins in the basement of the Provincial Office Building, he discovered his father's body (BFA 1989:190). Ch'oe Mi-ae, a twenty-four-year-old housewife, eight months pregnant, was standing in an alley near her home (near the entrance to the P'yŏnghwa Market, in front of Chŏnnam University) watching for her husband to come home when she was struck in the head by a bullet and killed (BFA 1989:273). Kim Chae-p'yŏng, a twenty-nine-year-old bureaucrat who had come to Kwangju to his in-laws' house because his wife was about to give birth, cowered with her in fear in their living room on the second floor as paratroopers, spread out in formation on the main road in Ssangch'on-dong, began firing at houses; a bullet pierced his lower jaw, and he later died (BFA 1989:296).

Throughout the afternoon demonstrators continued to seize weapons and strengthen their arsenal; they took arms from police stations and moved around the city and region in vehicles, getting guns. Soldiers and *simin'gun* started exchanging fire as citizens began organizing an armed defense. The numbers of those with weapons, however, remained relatively small. Lee Jae-eui records a gathering of about one hundred armed citizens downtown in the afternoon, dividing into groups of ten to twenty and preparing to protect strategic parts of the city. Although they included high school and college students, almost half were factory workers, small businessmen, clerks, and the unemployed. Their self-appointed leader was exhorting them: "People who are afraid to fight to the death should leave right now. Tonight we will fight the paratroopers to the last breath, until we win. We are people who will fight and not run away" (cited in

KMHRI 1990:331). The insurgents reportedly had three machine guns, which they planned to deploy around the city.

Late Wednesday afternoon the military forces remaining downtown began to withdraw. That evening, an outer ring of soldiers formed a perimeter around the city, occupying seven main roads and blockading Kwangju;[6] in the next days the casualties would be on the outskirts rather than the center of town. At 8 P.M. citizens confirmed the evacuation of the paratroopers from the city, and the insurgents finally took over the Provincial Office Building.

Democracy in Action

The Days of "Free Kwangju"

May 22

7:00 A.M.

It seems impossible to have such a lovely crisp blue dawn after a night of gunfire (some of it a little too close). Last night the Korean radio finally made mention of the "situation" here. They (whoever "they" are now—Communists and gangsters, says F[ather]) knocked over a couple of arsenals and got a lot of loot—not just weapons, but trucks and vehicles and explosives. The story (among others, I heard Kim Dae Jung had sought refuge with the American CIA and the Pres. of Chŏnnam Univ. had killed himself) was that the city was to be flooded with soldiers between 1 A.M. and 4 A.M., and be out at your own peril. Still no phones or transportation in or out of the city. So everyone is really scared. We all bedded down together in the main room—Yun-ok and I, Tong-nip, and Mother and Father. . . . Students whizzing through town on commandeered army trucks, horns blazing—full of courage. I don't know what to think of it all—especially since at a certain point people just get tired of explaining it to you in simple sentences. Plus so much is rumor.

Plus the undercurrents. F is for the status quo. M[other] feels. Yun- ok is scared and thinks of missing school (I sympathize most with this attitude). Poor Tong-nip is the saddest. Anyway, so we all bedded down. In the middle of the night M came over to tuck us in better—but I think she just wanted to hear other voices. The gunfire—including automatics—went on all night.

25

Never too close, I don't think. The sound of guns carries—esp. on a still,
clear night.

    Miller keeps urging me to get a bag packed—but I get stumped like
Mrs. Austin [another American, the wife of an exchange professor living at
Chŏnnam University]—am I going someplace else overnight? To Seoul for
the weekend? So I settle for keeping passport and money at hand. . . .

9:00 A.M.

    Well—the question is—who's got the guns? Miller says far from taking
the city last night, the soldiers got routed. Everything is closed—no food. But
M had the good sense to stock up on rice. A knot of neighbor women were con-
ferring in the sun. M said we can always eat your [the neighbors'] dogs! We'll
start with your house, then yours. . . . I think I shouldn't go out today—altho
I'd really like to know what the judges are saying, more than anything else.

    Miller says the French couple, plus some missionaries, are going to try
to make it out of town. Miller thinks we're crazy to have gotten trapped here;
I disagree. We could just as easily run to a mess as away from it.

10:00 A.M.

    A leaflet fluttered down on the roof. It only had the 3 points that the
radio gave the other night (says F in disgust), but I might as well translate
it. It is mostly in hanja *[Chinese characters]—sure to reach those elements*
they're appealing to.[1] In short:

> The ill-considered outbreak originating in the Kwangju
> area on the 18th is making it very hard to maintain the
> public peace.[2]

4:30

    Lovely weather. If you just looked out, it would seem nothing was going
on. I finally went out, but only as far as the corner. And talked to people. On
the one hand, it is a great way to get to know your neighbors. Plenty of knots
of women standing around. People are worried and tense—looking for infor-
mation. On the other side—I'm tense enough myself *not to want to deal with*
hostility. Also the atmosphere seems a little paranoid for idle chit chat. . . .

    People are frightened and concerned about the guns—but I don't hear
opposition to the government lessening. If anything, it is stiffening and the

mood is growing more sullen. Food is harder to come by—no stores open to-
day. . . . The phones and electricity still work.

> *I hear from Austin that the Huntleys report 15 dead and 100 wounded*
> *in the Presby hospital last night. Mostly from gunfire from the helicopter.*
> *That's only 1 hospital. This is the 5th day of blood in the streets. No riot is*
> *supposed to last this long. Are there really 200,000 citizens in the streets?*

> *Not one person has asked if anyone in the US would be worried about*
> *me. But lots of people are anxious to be assured that people in the US know*
> *what is going on. I can't figure the government's intention. On the one*
> *hand, waiting them out makes some sense. But—the longer you leave*
> *Kwangju self-governing—what do you risk (field journal, May 22, 1980)?*

ALTHOUGH IT WAS NOT YET CLEAR to cautious citizens still staying close
to their own front gates and afraid to venture out, the soldiers were indeed gone. Thursday, May 22, was the first day in a new stage in the uprising, the period of "*Kwangju haebang*" (Kwangju liberation). The
military's retreat was a tactical decision (Hwang Sŏk Yŏng 1985:131–
132). The *simin'gun* had captured 2,240 carbine rifles, 1,225 M-1 rifles,
12 38-caliber revolvers, 45 military pistols, 2 LMG machine guns,
46,400 rounds of ammunition, dozens of M-60 machine guns, 4 boxes
of TNT, many hand grenades, 100 detonators, 5 armored vehicles, and
many military vehicles, radios, and gas masks (Hwang Sŏk Yŏng
1985:130). Paratroopers defending the Provincial Office Building reportedly were being shelled by machine guns mounted on the roof of
the nearby Chŏnnam University Hospital (Hwang Sŏk Yŏng 1985:
126);[3] elsewhere defiant citizens were firing back, and, although the
simin'gun forces were much weaker than the Korean Army, more repression would surely lead to unacceptable levels of casualties on both
sides. The military assessment was that it would be better to isolate the
uprising in Kwangju and wait for the insurgents to cool down before
crushing them (Hwang Sŏk Yŏng 1985:132; Clark, ed. 1988:89).

On the morning of the 22d a group of fifteen citizens, including
religious leaders, students, and lawyers, joined with the vice governor
at the Provincial Office Building and established the 5.18 Kwangju Incident Settlement Committee (5.18 Kwangju Sat'ae Susŭp Taech'aek
Wiwŏnhoe) (KMHRI 1990:125). They debated about items for negotiation with the Martial Law Command, and at about 12:30, after several
hours of discussion, they decided on seven points:

1. Soldiers would not be sent back into the city until after the situation was resolved;
2. Release those who were detained;
3. Acknowledge the soldiers' excessive use of force;
4. No reprisals after the situation was resolved;
5. Amnesty for those who participated in the uprising;
6. Compensation for the deaths;
7. If the above conditions were met, citizens would disarm (KMHRI 1990:126).

Meanwhile, another group of influential citizens was also meeting that morning at Namdong Catholic Church. This gathering included "senior dissidents" (known for their prodemocracy, antigovernment views) and opposition figures concerned about how to deal with the situation. They agreed that among the members of the Incident Settlement Committee there were many who would not be reliable representatives of Kwangju's citizens, and they agonized over whether or not they should go to the Provincial Office Building to act together with them. The Namdong Church group heard about the seven points for negotiation, and its members eventually went to the Provincial Office Building, consulted with the Incident Settlement Committee already taking action there, and concurred with the agenda (KMHRI 1990:125).

Cho A-ra, the sixty-eight-year-old head of the YWCA, was present at the Namdong Church gathering, along with other well-respected older civic leaders, such as the lawyer Hong Nam-sun. Cho recounts the meeting that morning with the vice governor, at which she confronted him directly: "How on earth do you plan to get control of the present situation? We've come to hear your answer to this." Instead, the official appealed to them for suggestions: "I don't have any real alternatives. What should be done? If you have a good solution, please tell me." Cho replied that if the citizens had guns, probably the martial law forces would come back into Kwangju. Collecting the guns was the best they could do to give the military no pretext for returning. Cho volunteered to appeal to mothers, to take the lead in turning in the weapons. She also urged that demands include release of those in detention and the provision of funeral expenses to the families of the dead (cited in KCSPRI 1991:126–127).

At about 1 P.M. eight members of the Incident Settlement Committee went to the martial law branch office at the local military headquarters to negotiate. Of the seven demands, the authorities agreed only that if the guns were turned in, those who were detained would be released, and after the incident was resolved, there would be no retaliation. As to the rest of the points, they promised only to convey them to their superiors. The first negotiating session obtained just the release of prisoners; that day, 848 people were freed from custody (KMHRI 1990:126).

At 3 P.M. citizens spontaneously began gathering in front of the Provincial Office Building. At about 4 P.M. the representatives returned, and committee member Chang Hyu-dong reported the results of the meeting with the martial law authorities. The crowd concurred with "Prevent bloodshed" (Yuhyŏl pangji) and "Maintain order" (Chilsŏ yuji), but at the words "Let's collect the guns and turn them in" (Mugirŭl hoesuhayŏ pannaphaja), the audience responded with derision. Agitated citizens yelled "Don't trick us!" Chang quickly got off the platform, and the citizens' negotiation information meeting turned into an uprising rally (KMHRI 1990:126).[4]

Late in the afternoon, as the rally was breaking up, Kim Ch'anggil, a third-year student at Chŏnnam University, pointed out that "as students are responsible for this incident, we should be settling it" (cited in KMHRI 1990:125); about one hundred students gathered at the Namdo Art Hall and formed a fifteen-member Student Settlement Committee (Haksaeng Susŭp Taech'aek Wiwŏnhoe), with Kim as chair. That evening at the Provincial Office Building the students' committee, along with Professors Myŏng No-gŭn and Song Ki-suk, met and organized into sections to take care of such necessary tasks as weapons collection, vehicle control, maintenance and repair, public order, and medical care (KMHRI 1990:125).

May 23

8:00 A.M.

The Kwangju insurrection goes into its 6th day. Last night we all slept in the big room again, but it was probably unnecessary. No gunfire, and it is such a lovely day, again, it is hard to believe anything is going on out there. But the garbage piles up and the food goes down to rice and bean sprouts. Yesterday I contributed a can of carefully hoarded sardines. I'd like a bath. . . .

M just came in with the news that soldiers had tried once again to enter the city, from the airport side . . . but were repulsed by a big fire fight with students. AFKN finally said something—that students and the army were negotiating, and some students were turning in guns (this is what Tong-nip heard yesterday). They said about 40 dead—and the government was admitting to 9. . . .

You have to be proud to be from Kwangju—the only citizens with guts. Tong-nip says down here we have resistance in our blood. It may not rank up there with Tonghak [uprising of 1894], but. . . . The part I like best is how the helicopters can't fly over because they are afraid of getting shot down. And another thing—you have to hand it to universal military training. I can't imagine many US students would have the vaguest idea how to engage in urban guerilla war (who knows how to shoot a gun?).

M reports the house behind has had several deaths.

9:00 A.M.

Miller called with his daily news bulletin. Says 16 out of 20 gun [counties] in Chŏnnam [Chŏlla Nam Do Province] have armed citizens—Mokp'o [city] is like Kwangju. . . . According to Miller, negotiations are going on regarding compensation for death and property damage, etc.

9:00 P.M.

I've been unsuccessfully tying knots all day—almost none have come out. It seems to be quiet out. I'll sleep in my own place. In fact, the usual noisy drunken crew is going by outside—life may be getting back to normal. Drunken revelers—I never thought I'd welcome the sound. Miller is going to try to walk out tomorrow; failing that, he'll try to go out with a German camera crew. He also clued me to what KBS is now saying: that Wickham [General John A.Wickham, U.S. commander-in-chief, Combined Forces Command] sent the soldiers into Kwangju! . . . I told the family it wasn't so, and they immediately got on spreading the word. KBS is still saying 4 dead—when this A.M. 52 coffins were spread out by the Toch'ŏng (field journal, May 23, 1980).

In the afternoon Mother and I went out to walk around downtown. Despite the fact that that morning hundreds of middle and high school students had been working to clean up the streets (KCSPRI 1991:289), Kwangju still looked (in my words at the time) "a bit trashed." Many small government buildings and offices, especially police stations, were gutted. A few other buildings looked like they had been attacked and had bent grates and showed signs of fire. We went by the International Telegraph and Telephone Office, which was boarded up but not damaged. There were crashed and burned vehicles—mostly city buses and army jeeps. I saw one overturned mailbox, and the sidewalks were ripped up, turned into hurling stones, the preferred weapons of demonstrators.

On that day and the ones that followed, I never saw any evidence of looting or destruction of private property. Although the government was announcing this was a riot of "impure elements"—Communists, thugs, and criminals, who posed a danger to citizens who ventured out—it was clear that with the withdrawal of government troops, Kwangju's streets were once again safe. The turmoil and terror of the previous week were gone, replaced by a kind of festive civic pride and communal resolve. In the years since 1980 (as we shall see), the public orderliness and calm, atmosphere of cooperation, and remarkable lack of crime that characterized the "Free Kwangju" period is often evoked as one of the most important aspects of the *"Kwangju chŏngsin"* (Kwangju spirit). While it is easy to dismiss the model of a self-governing Kwangju as a kind of fantasy, a euphoric myth that remains forever untested by time—after all, the institutions of the central government were back in place a short while later, and there was an unreality, an air of suspended animation, about those days—public order, not chaos, prevailed.

There was no traffic on the streets but motorcycles and bicycles. In 1980 few private citizens owned cars (and the ones who did, the wealthy, used them to get out of town); in addition, the Student Settlement Committee had set up a system of numbering vehicles and controlling (and/or appropriating) their use in an effort to conserve gasoline (KMHRI 1990:333). But there were lots of pedestrians—many in suits, women with babies on their backs, all milling about, greeting friends, exchanging information.[5]

There was a big crowd around the fountain in the plaza in front of the Provincial Office Building; a platform had been set up, and students were addressing the crowd through megaphones. Throughout the first days the fighting had focused on the Provincial Office Building as the symbolic center of governmental authority in Kwangju; during the days of "Free Kwangju" crowds naturally converged around the fountain in front of the white, three-story building that was now *simin'gun* headquarters. People came searching for information about loved ones or just to find out what was going on. A makeshift morgue had been set up in the basement, with about fifty corpses; high school girls were put to work washing the bodies and escorting distraught family members there to identify them. Handwritten notices and lists were pasted up; I saw one that listed the number of dead (seventy people) at one of the local hospitals.

In 1997 the area in front of the Provincial Office Building was formally named the 5.18 Democracy Plaza (5.18 Minju Kwangjang); a small plaque in the wall around the building bears the new designation. The plaza (really a traffic circle around the fountain) remains the emotional and political heart of Kwangju. In 1996, it was one of the sites on the "5.18 Sacred Places Pilgrimage" tour (5.18 Sŏngji Sullye);[6] a pamphlet outlining the circuit describes the events that occurred there and on Kŭmnamno, the main thoroughfare that runs into it. Now in May during the Uprising anniversary, the streets are often blocked off and events are held in the plaza. On May 17, a large sound stage is set up in front of the fountain, facing Kŭmnamno, for the Uprising Eve celebration. The plaza remains a favorite destination for student protests and demonstrations. During the seventeenth anniversary events in 1997, students battled nightly with riot police around the plaza, and the area was blocked off as frequently with police cordons—to keep radical students out—as with traffic barricades to create a pedestrian mall for the festivities.

In 1980, the Incident Settlement Committee, reorganized and expanded to include college students, met at noon, again to consider points for negotiation. The group was sharply divided; on the one hand, some were saying, "Let's collect the guns and turn them in," while others asked how just returning the weapons, with no guarantees, would avenge those who had already died. This faction wanted to wait until the government showed good faith, by granting some of the citizens' requests, before disarming the *simin'gun* (KMHRI 1990:126; also Hwang Sŏk Yŏng 1985:160–162). The committee drew up another list of demands:

1. Acknowledge excessive use of force by paratroopers and martial law forces;
2. Release those who have been detained;
3. Martial law forces will not reenter the city;
4. Prohibit reprisals and punishment of citizens and students;
5. Pay compensation to dead and injured;
6. Give truthful reports and broadcasts;
7. Stop using provocative language;
8. Reopen transportation. (KMHRI 1990:126).

By then, about one thousand weapons had been turned in (Hwang Sŏk Yŏng 1985:161), and some members of the committee exchanged two hundred guns with the regional martial law command for thirty-four prisoners (KMHRI 1990:126).

At 3 P.M., about one hundred thousand people gathered around the fountain for the Che 1 Ch'a Minju Suho Pŏmsimin Kwŏlgi Taehoe (First All-Citizens' Uprising Rally to Protect Democracy), the beginning of a daily series of rallies led by young political activists. According to Lee Jae-eui, after the massive spontaneous rally the previous day, students and activists distressed at the Incident Settlement Committee's conciliatory stance took the initiative in planning and organizing these public demonstrations as a means of expressing popular sentiments. These rallies "in the midst of the Kwangju Uprising, during the days of the people's liberation, consolidated the insurgents' will to fight and gave birth to a new leadership that could give it shape. These mass rallies were the only means of reaching a broad consensus in favor of democratic protections and the right to life; they were a productive form of direct democratic process that served to clarify popular opinion." Lee goes on to assert that "Young students had no particular problem with continuing the struggle. But ordinary citizens, and most of the masses, participated in armed resistance out of individual feelings, rather than systematically, in accordance with some unifying principle. Thus the risk grew that some of the prominent people [on the Incident Settlement Committee] could distort these people's demands. It was essential to secure unity and solidarity in action through the mass rallies" (Hwang Sŏk Yŏng 1985:167).

Mother and I ended our circuit of the downtown area that day at the market, which was open on a somewhat ad hoc basis. I took it as a good sign that there were fresh vegetables available, if at a high price. Then we went home, and although I was glad to have gone out, I also felt glad to be back.

While it was safe on May 23 to go freely about in Kwangju, the sudden, random violence continued at the edge of town and in the surrounding countryside as the army, now positioned outside the city, tried to prevent the uprising from spreading to the nearby counties. And *simin'gun* did shoot down a reconnaissance helicopter at Paegundong, killing three soldiers (KCSPRI 1991:290). Two well-known massacres also occurred on May 23, both several kilometers outside of Kwangju, on the way to Hwasun. The first happened in the morning, and the memorial record of one of the victims gives this account:

> Ms. Kim Ch'un-nye [eighteen years old], who was a factory worker at the Ilsin Textile Co., had to go to her hometown of Hwasun for her grandfather's memorial rites on May 23. Kim Ch'un-nye, who went to the city with her dormitory mate Ko Yŏng-ja, was uncertain what to do. Given that telephone lines outside the city had already been cut, there was no chance that suburban buses were still running. She went to the Provincial Office Building and told her story to a citizens' militia member, asking as a favor if they would take her to Hwasun. So the two factory women got on a vehicle with nine citizens' militia members and headed for Hwasun. When they got one kilometer beyond Chunam village at Chiwon-dong, where the paratroopers were staying, suddenly from the hills in both directions bullets rained down. The citizens' militia members in the vehicle stopped the car and raised their hands, yelling, "Don't shoot!," but the gunfire from the martial law soldiers lying in ambush on the opposite hill did not stop. The two factory women and nine citizens' militia members traveling in the vehicle were all killed on the spot.
>
> Family members were able to identify Kim Ch'un-nye's body five days later at the Chŏnnam University Hospital. The woman's body, which had started to decompose, was ghastly, like some torn up rag. The woman, whose body had been struck by 11 bullets, and especially her lower abdomen, was pierced with bullet wounds. The M-16 bullets that pierced her chest made a 12 cm exit wound in her back. Her face and hair were a bloody mess because they had dragged her through the hills. Already her back and torso were swarming with maggots (BFA 1989:232).

The second episode, now known as the "Chunam Maŭl Yang-min Haksal" (the Chunam Village Massacre of Innocents), is more fully recorded because of the testimony of Hong Kŭm-suk, a sixteen-year-old high school girl who was the sole survivor. When she described the incident at the National Assembly hearings in 1988, it was the first time her family had heard the details of that day (KMHRI 1990:971). She had been evacuated from the scene by military helicopter and treated, then detained and interrogated for one hundred days afterward, and she had been warned never to discuss what had happened. According to Hong,

> 1980.5.23 between two and three in the afternoon the bus I took left Kwangju and headed toward Hwasun. About 18 male and female students were in the 25-passenger minibus (2 high school girls, 2 young women, and 14 male students). The male students were armed with M-1s and carbines—and in the vehicle there were 2-way radios. They seemed to know each other well, and they said they had gone here and there getting planks for coffins.
>
> I had gotten on the bus in the vicinity of Kwangju Park. In the morning I had come to Kwangju with my mother to look for my two brothers, who were students at Chŏnnam University and High School, and after going all around, I had even become separated from my mother, and while heading home on foot, I had met up with the bus. At that time traffic within the city was at a standstill; somebody said that this bus was heading toward my house, and so I got on. Our home was in the vicinity of Okch'ŏn Girls' Commercial High School in Chuwŏl-dong, which is on the road to Naju.
>
> But in the neighborhood of the Taech'ang gas station in Wŏlsan-dong, the bus suddenly changed directions. I asked why, and they said they were going to stop someplace else first, and they went toward Naju. So I didn't get off; I just kept riding.
>
> Pak Hyŏn-suk, a third-year Girls' High School student, and I introduced ourselves, and I sat down in the very back row of seats.
>
> When the bus passed Kwangju stream and was almost out of Chiwŏn-dong, a soldier standing by the side of the road gave a signal to stop. Because we all knew what would happen if we stopped, the vehicle speeded up. With sudden noisy sounds, bullets poured down on the bus. Bullets kept coming down, and someone yelled to turn

the bus around. The moment the vehicle was turned around, the driver was hit by a bullet, and he fell forward, bleeding.

The young people in the bus who were facing the mountains pushed out their gun barrels and started returning fire. So more bullets poured down.

After awhile, one young man, judging the situation impossible, said, "We have to stop shooting and raise our guns in surrender." Male students waved their guns, and the female students waved two hands and handkerchiefs, yelling, "Don't shoot!" But the paratroopers did not stop the flood of bullets. Usually the bullets were coming from the front and back part of the bus. I, sitting in the far back row, moved to the middle and got under a seat. The deafening sound of guns, the screams begging for life, moaning, and the sound of bullets ricocheting off the back of the bus—such sounds created hellish confusion inside the bus.

A male student who was shot, his intestines spilling out on the floor of the bus, was saying, "I want to live." He suddenly closed his eyes and rolled over like he was dead. I closed my eyes and rolled over like I was dead. In a moment the sound of gunfire stopped, and we couldn't even hear the sound of people moaning. I felt nervous, with pains all over my body, and I opened my eyes. I was bleeding all over, including my right arm and back and sides and thighs. Luckily, I had not been hit directly by bullets, but splinters were all over my body.

Voices came from nearby. Soldiers said, "Let's make sure they are all dead." Three or four soldiers came inside the bus. They nudged people with their boots to see if they were alive or dead. From someone in the back came a voice saying, "I want to live." After pulling that person out, the soldiers went back in the bus and there was another sound.

"If you want to survive, don't be afraid and get up." And from a person in the front came a moaning sound, begging for life. "Bring him! Let's make a complete check!"

I was lying on my back like I was dead, and I was glancing at them sideways. Then suddenly a soldier's boot kicked me in the side, and it was painful, so I let out a sound. So when they checked if everyone was dead again, an ambulance came and gave me simple first aid. And I was taken into the mountains by a farmer's tractor (KMHRI 1990:970–971).

Hong goes on to relate that she was taken with two male survivors—one severely injured, the other begging for his life—to someone in authority. The commanding officer ordered the others shot; she is presumed to be the only one who lived.

Meanwhile, in Seoul, the United States had made a public announcement on May 22 expressing "deep concern" over the civil strife in Kwangju and warning North Korea not to try to take advantage of the situation. The U.S. government has subsequently stated that despite assurances by the Korean military authorities that this announcement would be broadcast and air-dropped in Kwangju (and indeed leaflets were printed), this was never done. In fact, U.S. officials later discovered that instead the media were reporting that the United States had approved the dispatch of the Special Warfare Command troops to Kwangju (USIS 1989:16–17).

[margin note: Korean media takes advantage of US in media broadcasts]

The United States has repeatedly denied allegations of complicity in the Kwangju massacre, stating that as the paratroopers were not under Combined Forces Command control, it is absurd to suggest that General Wickham approved their deployment. However, the United States did release the Twentieth Division in light of the argument by Korean military authorities that it would be preferable to use soldiers from this division (which was trained in riot control) rather than the paratroopers in Kwangju; on May 20 the United States was notified of the movement of soldiers of the Twentieth Division to Kwangju (USIS 1989:16).

As it turns out, declassified documents published in 1996 by the journalist Tim Shorrock (the "Cherokee Papers") suggest that U.S. military intelligence was aware in early May 1980 that the Special Warfare Command units were on nationwide alert and that the Seventh Brigade was probably targeted for use in Kwangju in the event of student unrest (Shorrock 1996:1A). Shorrock (1999) (and others) claim that Korean Martial Law Command disinformation aside, U.S. officials were far better informed of—and even involved in—the Korean military's suppression of dissent in the spring of 1980 than they have ever been willing to admit.

[margin note: is this forgivable given the Iran fiasco?]

May 24

The Seventh Day of the Kwangju Insurrection. Nice day, but a little cooler and getting overcast. The rose—a huge one—bloomed in the garden. There was weapons fire between about 2:30 and 3:30 A.M.; otherwise, all was quiet. M and I were about to go out and do a look around when we got some news, from F's grapevine (we have 4 going, quite efficiently now—F, TN [Tong-nip], me, and M goes out and scouts). It seems the rep[resentative]s of the students (4) and citizens (6) couldn't reach agreement with the soldiers, so the soldiers are about to have another go at the city. So much for going out—things are supposed to start getting bad again at noon. I found out that Miller made it out okay and is now on his way to Seoul to talk to the Ambassador. . . .

It seems to me that if the soldiers come in again today, either they get the shit kicked out of them or there will be quite a bloodbath. The mood is far from wanting to give up. But if they wait a few days, the situation may defuse itself. Or that's what I think. . . .

12:30

Why aren't we going out? says father. Well, it isn't because we are afraid— we aren't, anymore. In fact, the downtown is safe right now and stores are open. The problem is that the authorities (i.e., the guys in the planes [dropping leaflets on the city]) are saying to stay inside. So if we go out, people will see us, and when this is all over, we'll be accused of having taken part. . . .

4:30

Went to [a friend's], talked, and came back safely; [things are] more "normal," but not so many stores open as I had expected. Still, tension is lessening. The citizens had been given an ultimatum—12:00 the arms had to be given back. It was extended until 6. We'll see what happens. . . .

It is harder and harder to do things. I tie and retie knots. I read some. I talk to the family. I can't write letters. I can't study. I don't even want to think about my project. . . .

7:00 P.M.

It's raining. People worry that the students will get wet and chilled. The word is—the students say that they'll be killed whether they give up their guns or not, so why give them up. Right on. I think popular sentiment is with them (field journal, May 24, 1980).

The military had announced in a radio broadcast at 8:00 A.M. that if people surrendered their weapons, the Martial Law Command would not bring charges against them (Hwang Sŏk Yŏng 1985:171). But trust, of both Chun Doo Hwan and the Choi Kyu-ha interim government, as well as among the various groups in Kwangju working for some resolution to the uprising, was in short supply. Fear of an army blitzkrieg to retake the city was palpable, and the rumors of imminent attack were constant. Leaflets floated down from military helicopters, warning that the uprising was the work of *kochŏng kanch'ŏp* (North Korean spies), *pulsunbuja* (impure elements), and *kkangp'ae* (hooligans) and threatening army intervention (Hwang Sŏk Yŏng 1985:165). The mood of triumphant defiance was giving way to uncertainty and to acrimonious debate over the appropriate course: surrender or continued resistance.

In the morning, the Incident Settlement Committee, which was still working to dissuade the *simin'gun* from further armed resistance, had collected more than 50 percent of the weapons (Hwang Sŏk Yŏng 1985:170); it also printed up and circulated the results of its meeting with martial law authorities the previous day:

1. There would be no military presence in the city;
2. The military would admit there had been excessive use of force;
3. Of the 927 arrested, the military would free all but 79;
4. The government would complete preparations for compensation and would have medical treatment plans ready;
5. The military would make efforts to encourage objective news coverage;
6. The military would not use terms like "impure elements" or "rioting mobs" to describe the people of Kwangju;
7. The military will allow unarmed civilians to enter and leave the city;
8. The military promises that there will be no retaliation (CSPRI 1988: 124).

In retrospect, of course, optimism about these bargaining points seems pitifully naive. After May 27, Kwangju resembled an armed camp, and when I left Korea in mid-October, buses traveling into the city were still routinely being checked. About 2,500 people were arrested, some 640 stood trial in military court, and 389 were convicted (KCS 1997:152). As noted above, public discussion of 5.18 was banned in South Korea throughout most of the 1980s, and despite the National Assembly hearings in 1988 and the public trials of Roh Tae Woo and Chun Doo Hwan in 1996, the feeling remains strong in Kwangju that the "truth" of May 1980 is still not established. It was years before the government finished paying compensation to the victims, and for many of the seriously wounded, adequate medical treatment continues to be an issue.[7] The Uprising touched the lives of most of Kwangju's citizens; it is not surprising that a slogan on a banner at the May 1997 anniversary events would still proclaim that "The May problem is not over" (5 wŏl munjenŭn kkŭt' naji anatta).

In the afternoon of Saturday, May 24, 1980, tens of thousands of people once again thronged the fountain plaza in front of the Provincial Office Building, where the Second All-Citizens' Uprising Rally was held. One of the most important points to be made about 5.18 is its "popular" nature. It was my observation at the time—since supported by other evidence—that participation in the event was citywide and involved a majority of the population. By "participation" I mean the performance at some point in the ten days of a public action demonstrating support for the uprising, be it appearing at one of the rallies, giving food or money to the *simin'gun*, engaging in street fighting, negotiating with the military, or procuring and bearing arms. I heard no opposition to the uprising. Even those who chose to leave the city seem to have done so more from fear or to avoid the appearance of participation (disassociating themselves from the event), rather than from disagreement with the sentiments of the rebellious populace. Also I am not aware of any anti- or counterrebellion incidents (other than the activities of government agents, provocateurs, and infiltrators), and there was no violence among rival groups of citizens.[8] Disagreements between the more radical activists and student leaders and the more moderate Incident Settlement Committee were over tactical matters in dealing with the military, rather than over the fundamental "righteousness" of the citizens' armed resistance.

Actually, so widespread was mass support for the uprising that the more interesting question would be who did *not* participate and why. There were those, like the father in my household, who were initially constrained from acting on the basis of a common vested interest in not being labeled as revolutionaries. In this category are those, primarily government employees (judges, civil servants, school administrators—mostly men in positions of public trust) who were afraid of losing their jobs. When the inevitable end to the uprising came and the government regained control, if they were known to have demonstrated (they reasoned), their positions would be in jeopardy.

These people were the last to show their support publicly for the uprising, but in the end, many of them did join the rallies downtown when the nonviolent demonstrations numerically reached their peak. One thing that served to involve the rest of the citizens (especially that category of initially reluctant participants) and helps explain what kept people in the streets and strengthened the sense of resistance within the city was the emergence of a new grievance during the days of "Free Kwangju." That grievance was (and to some extent still is) the government's refusal to apologize or in any way to accept responsibility for provoking the initial violence. Rebellious citizens took to the streets as a defensive response to the repressive actions of the military, and they remained in the streets when the government labeled them hooligans, outlaws, and Communists for doing so.

At the mass rally on May 24, there was public pressure on the Incident Settlement Committee; citizens who feared they would be sold out in an unconditional surrender to the government demanded the dissolution of the group. Angry and dissatisfied demonstrators claimed that the negotiating stance of the committee did not represent the will of Kwangju citizens (Hwang Sŏk Yŏng 1985:171–174). And (needless to say) the demands did not include any of the popular aspirations displayed on banners hung up around the fountain plaza: "Long live democratic citizens!" "Fight to the death!" "Let's get rid of the remnants of Yusin!" "Let's tear the murderer Chun Doo Hwan apart!" "Guarantee workers' rights!" "End martial law!" "Release Kim Dae Jung!" (Hwang Sŏk Yŏng 1985:158).

A survey of Kwangju citizens in 1988 suggests not only that the approval rating for the work of the Incident Settlement Committee was low, but also that most people in Kwangju were unaware of its activities. About one-third of the respondents knew nothing about the committee, while another third had heard of it but did not know what it was doing; fewer than 10 percent felt well informed about the committee's role. Only about 21 percent felt that the committee had done a good job (PJC 1988:30–31).

According to one source, the committee itself worked to sabotage the gathering that afternoon, cutting off the electricity for the public address system (Hwang Sŏk Yŏng 1985:172). An open "Appeal to the Nation's Democratic Citizens" was read, and an effigy of Chun Doo Hwan was burned (see CSPRI 1988:120–122; Hwang Sŏk Yŏng 1985:

174; A. Peterson 1995:231). Rain interrupted the rally, and that night wet *simin'gun* began leaving their posts and turning in their weapons.

On the outskirts of town, the random violence continued. Another well-known incident, the Massacre of Innocents at Chinwŏl-dong (Chinwŏldong Yangmin Haksal), occurred on the afternoon of May 24 at a reservoir. This is what the memorial record says of one child's death:

On May 24, Pang Kwang-bŏm [aged twelve], a first-year student at Chŏnnam Middle School, was bathing with his friends in the Wŏnjae village reservoir in Songam-dong. It was when the paratroopers who had been staying at Chiwŏn-dong, brutally slaughtering citizens passing between Kwangju and Hwasun, were retreating to the Songjŏng airport to prepare for the military assault on the Provincial Office Building at dawn on May 27. While passing through Chinwŏl-dong, the paratroopers, who had to retreat on mountain trails from Hak-dong to Songam-dong, began opening fire on houses.

Hearing gunshots, some ten children who were bathing quickly ran away. The soldiers passing the reservoir indiscriminately fired at the children who were still bathing. Pang Kwang-bŏm, who was the last to flee, was hit by a bullet in the left side of his head. Kwang-bŏm, who was shot just two meters short of the flood gate behind which he hoped to hide, had as much as 18 by 16 cm of his head blown off by the bullet that hit him.

Children who, despite the grim situation in Kwangju, were just playing, bathing in the reservoir! To the paratroopers firing at random, was even Kwang-bŏm, an innocent seventh grader, a rioter and "impure element"? And for cows as well—valuable property in the countryside—can the soldiers also invoke the right of self-defense?[9]

Pang Kwang-bŏm's death, with half his head blown away, happened because he was living in Kwangju. Afterward, his father, Pang Tu-hyŏng, who had embraced his eldest son's corpse and rolled on the floor kicking and screaming like the world had collapsed, could not pass a day without drinking and finally, unable to get over his son's gruesome death, became mentally deranged.

The reason Kwangju continues is that we can never put aside these deaths as some past misfortune; now this death must be the fertilizer for real democratization (BFA 1989:270).

May 25

Day 8 of the Kwangju insurrection. Rainy all day long. The expected gunfire in the night didn't come. Kwangju has become a media event, and all the foreigners were out today. M and I went down early to the prov. office. The safest day yet—lots and lots of people. The funeral was supposed to be at 3. They had the bodies in the gym [Sangmugwan] and were letting family members in to see them. Normal people out today—men in suits, lots of women. M saw lots of her friends ("So-and-so's daughter died." —"Oh, no, the one who lives [at] such-and-such?" —"Yes. But wasn't she young?" — "Yes, only about 3d year middle school.") And so it went, M picking up bits and pieces all around, and I doing the same. I got interviewed for French TV—they were really nice. I got crowds all around me. People saying—tell them how it happened, the first days, what the soldiers did. That is concern one: does the world know what it was that radicalized us? Then point 2 is— tell them we are led by law-abiding people, not gangs roaming the streets. We evidently are big news, and have been. M dragged me over to talk to a blasé CBS cameraman. . . . I had lots of questions for him, but I don't think he knew shit. No, the rest of the country is not demonstrating. Yes, the US govt is firmly supporting Chun. People clamored to have me ask what the world thought of Kwangju. . . .

I did pick up lots of news, all told. A group of clergy put the body count at 172, with over 800 injured. New rumors—Chun isn't strong enough to come in. Chun is just waiting to come in. Nothing is going on in the rest of the country. Oh, the funeral itself. Well. It didn't really happen. It turned into a rally. They had 52 bodies there—from one hospital? Supposedly only 1/3 dead were students. The whole square and more was filled. People all over. M said—surely one from every house. Military vehicles manned by students in makeshift, semi-uniform. We sang songs, heard speeches. Then it started to rain, so we came home, stopping first at the market, which is getting better, but still limited. [The] egg lady says [it is] still hard to get goods in. M got a chicken. . . .

Got home to find F had stolen all my hot water for his own bath. Had a long political discussion with Tong-nip. I just don't know at all what will happen. I can't believe it has lasted this long. I don't know how it could end. People have cleaned the place up, order seems to be holding. Students have up signs: the eyes of the world are on us, so behave yourselves and don't mess it up. The missionaries say 95% of the weapons have been turned in to the students.[10] Will this deteriorate into a farce? Who knows. I think something has to happen.

Well, [I] just took a break to go in and listen to the President on the 9 P.M. news. It is just like with Nixon—everyone sits around and snorts and boos and says—the bastard. They had pictures of Kwangju—but all misrepresentative. Focusing on the trucks of students. Showing empty streets, and saying people were afraid they would be killed if they went out. . . . We are so used to saying what we want down here, it is hard to get paranoid again. On the streets, I kept forgetting to be careful about what I was saying. I am sure people were wandering around, checking up, trying to listen and remember. I should be careful (field journal, May 25, 1980).

At 11:30 last night [May 25] . . . I was awakened by a call from a captain at the US base. I have a statement to read to you, he says. The foreign ministry called all the embassies to have them get their people out of Kwangju. The US embassy wants me out. He reads his piece, then we talk—just how am I supposed to get out? We discuss walking. He says—ask any soldier (Korean) for directions—they will help you. Here we see his comprehension of this situation revealed. He says the Petersons [an American missionary family] will get the Austins out. So. Well, do they [U.S. embassy officials] expect anything [bad to happen]? Hard to say. It seems they fear hostages. At this point I really crack up. So I call the Austins, who had not been called. . . . I discuss it with M and F. They agree with my assessment that if the missionaries go, I have to take it seriously. We discuss the fact that the govt may be trying to scare the populace. Or to make sure we don't talk. How can they pretend it is dangerous when we all stay and deny it? Or maybe everyone is just doing a pro forma hand washing. I decide to sleep on it (field journal, May 26, 1980).

On Sunday, May 25, the citywide joint funeral once again was postponed; the coffins remained in the Sangmugwan. Mother and I, out in the morning to look around, went back in the afternoon for what turned out to be the third uprising rally.

By this time, the split between the "soft-line" Incident Settlement Committee and Student Committee and the more radical "hard-line" activists was serious, and the Settlement Committee was on the verge of collapse. Although the moderates still kept persuading *simin'gun* to turn in their weapons, by May 25 the lines were more firmly drawn; no more guns were being given up, and the activists were planning to take over the leadership of the uprising (Hwang Sŏk Yŏng 1985:183–186).

At 10:00 in the morning, a meeting was held at the YMCA between the senior dissidents and the young activists to try to reach some agreement. The senior dissidents argued in favor of surrendering the weapons to prevent further bloodshed. To the youthful insurgents, this represented a betrayal of all they had been fighting for. In general, the older group either opposed the uncompromising position of the *simin'gun* or was indifferent (KMHRI 1990:126).

That same day, at 2:00 P.M., the meeting continued at the Namdong Church. Finally, the senior dissidents decided that in the interests of presenting a united front in negotiating with the military, they should join with the Incident Settlement Committee at the Provincial Office Building. They went there, and as a newly enlarged Settlement Committee (with twenty-five members), the group issued another set of resolutions:

1. The government should acknowledge that the Kwangju incident was caused by the government's excessive use of force;
2. The government should publicly apologize and ask forgiveness;
3. Compensation must be paid to all victims;
4. It must be made clear that there would be no reprisals (KMHRI 1990:126–127).

That evening there was a meeting of the Student Settlement Committee. After fierce debate, the leader, Kim Ch'ang-gil, resigned, and those who were resolved to fight to the end formed a new leadership group, renamed the Citizens and Students Struggle Committee (Simin Haksaeng T'ujang Wiwŏnhoe).

On Sunday, May 25, at 7:00 P.M., KBS evening news announced that the Provincial Office Building had fallen into the hands of the hard-liners (Hwang Sŏk Yŏng 1985:191). That same evening, President Choi Kyu-ha visited the regional Martial Law Command; his special statement was later aired three times on KBS. In it, he warned that "For the youths who took up arms in momentary excitement and anger, it is still not too late to give up your weapons and go home. As we are all brothers, members of the same nation, there is no problem we cannot resolve through dialogue. . . . Let's not forget that without a doubt the Communists in the North will exploit our confrontation" (as cited in Hwang Sŏk Yŏng 1985:196).

According to a U.S. government statement on Kwangju issued in 1989, on May 24 General Wickham was informed that the Martial Law Command had finalized plans to reenter and retake the city. Wickham urged restraint and "reported to Washington that the likelihood of Martial Law Command forces having to reenter Kwangju was low because both he and [Ambassador William] Gleysteen believed that the Citizens' Committee was having some success at calming the situation" (USIS 1989:18). The next day, however, the U.S. government began receiving "ominous signals"; the Korean Foreign Ministry asked on May 25 that all foreigners leave Kwangju (which is, I assume, why I was called), presumably in anticipation of further army action and increased violence, and Korean military authorities began to say "[that] hard-core radical students had taken over the city, that their demands were excessive, and that they did not seem interested in good faith negotiations" (USIS 1989:18).

The U.S. government reports that ninety-one foreign nationals (from the United States, Canada, Italy, Great Britain, and South Africa) gathered at the Kwangju air base and that twenty-three of them were evacuated by the U.S. Air Force on May 26 (USIS 1989:18). However, it is my impression that most of the foreign residents I encountered downtown on May 25—Americans teaching at local universities, missionaries, a few Peace Corps Volunteers, and even a German national I had never met before—chose, like me, to stay. Arnold Peterson has written that the remaining members of the American missionary community (many had already sent family members out) agreed in discussions on May 25, and again the next morning, that to leave at that point would betray the commitment they had earlier made to "see this through along with the people of Kwangju" (A. Peterson 1995:235).

There were other good reasons for staying as well. Mother, perusing the crowds on May 26, noted that it was good so many people were out: "they can't do anything if the streets are full." I felt much less sanguine. Standing among masses of people around the fountain plaza during the days of "Free Kwangju," I could not help glancing nervously upward; I believed the Korean military was certainly capable of strafing the crowds from airplanes. The danger to my personal safety lay not downtown, among Kwangju citizens, but outside at the perimeter, where Korean army units were massing to retake the city. On May 25, the idea of walking to the outskirts of Kwangju to seek refuge with "friendly" Korean troops struck me as ludicrous.

The journalist Terry Anderson recounts watching the final assault on May 27 from a small hotel behind the Provincial Office Building. Crouching at a window to take a picture, he was spotted by two soldiers on top of the building who "then opened up with their M-16s." Anderson says, "We had believed the government knew this hotel was occupied by foreign press, but either no one had told the soldiers or they didn't care" (Anderson 1997:11). It was to be expected; while the reentering forces were supposedly from the regular army (Twentieth Division), it was the vicious paratroopers, wearing regular army uniforms of the Twentieth Division to disguise their identity, who led the last attack on the Provincial Office Building, as well as other strategic locations (USIS 1989:19).

May 26

5:00 P.M.

Day nine of the insurrection. A full day. . . . M and I went out on our reconnaissance mission—getting to be a regular routine, and it works out really well. We buck each other up and she is a natural snoop. She stops, talks to people, asks questions I wouldn't ask. Lots of info from her. Example: we walked to the court along the tracks (no trains, remember.) Lots of traffic in both directions. She asked people where they were going. It is one of the main routes in and out. (People coming in are older, with children in the city. Going out—we passed some groups. . . . High school students being sent or going to country homes, since no school.) No one at the court—in fact, kids playing in the front. As we came up, the govt side dropped more flyers—what do they say? Don't bother—the usual govt crap. . . . We were torn where to look first. . . . A group of students—from Mokp'o, we heard— was marching around town (M wanted to follow them). Then downtown, too. As many—no, more than yesterday. And different types. Every day more venture out. Yesterday, more respectable people and young school girls in uniform. (Many going to and from church.) Today—many, many more middle-aged, middle-class "respectable" men. I saw a few more from court.

And students—more college students who have been in hiding, down to see the bodies. M and I went in [to the memorial service] . . . .

[After the memorial service] M and I walk on, into the market. More out today—more stores than just food are open for business, and stuff like eggs has made it into town. Still no fresh meat/fish, though. As we leave, the green paddy wagon van—of the sort used to bring criminals to court every day—pulls up with its two funeral wreaths on the front (it is known as the body van, as that has been its use). Out hops a student in fatigues, carrying handcuffs, and walks off through the market. What is he doing? Maybe out to catch thieves? That is what was said at first, but, no—soon we all find out. Three more students hop out and also disappear into the market. It is the funeral delegation, collecting money. In five minutes they have a huge wad of 1,000 W notes (M and I estimate—150,000 W). They are not urging people—in fact, it is hard to get their attention to contribute. People are pushing money on them. And they are very polite and are saying—it is not for us, it is for funeral expenses. And they also write down names and contributions. And home we come, yak yak with friends, to report. M says we have to go downtown, otherwise how can we meet our friends? Something of a social occasion—yes—but also seen as a statement of support. We'll go out again tomorrow. . . .

Where are the troops? Evidently they are ringing the city, and made an attempt to move closer, but were reminded they promised not to. AFKN says they are closing in, taking control of the countryside. [Norm] Thorpe says the citizens' committee is acting as sort of a middle group between the soldiers and students. But the problem still seems to be that the government is not properly repentant about events. It hasn't admitted it wantonly killed people. It hasn't said it feels sorry for the tragic events—no admitting Kwangju may have had just cause. It keeps saying the citizens of Kwangju are outlaws. This seems to be the rub. Now, the deadline . . . is midnight (field journal, May 26, 1980).

Of course, mother and I did not go out together around the city the next day or for many days afterward. Monday, May 26, was the last day of "Free Kwangju," although that was not clear that morning. I was awakened at 7:00 A.M. by a call from Norm Thorpe, a journalist for the *Asian Wall Street Journal* who had promised Mark Peterson that he would check up on me. He came by to look at my city maps, talk to my family, and pass on what he knew.

At 5:30 A.M. a tank column had headed into the city from the army hospital to the Rural Development Office; it was stopped when a group of seventeen members of the Incident Settlement Committee, keeping an all-night vigil at the Provincial Office Building, walked to meet it (KMHRI 1990:127). Committee members quickly mobilized a street demonstration, reportedly even lying down on the road in front of the tanks (Hwang Sŏk Yŏng 1985:198). Negotiations between the Martial Law Command and the committee members continued in hopes of a peaceful resolution. In the morning, the fourth citywide rally was held. The new leadership held a press conference with foreign correspondents and, in the afternoon, met with the mayor to present a list of requests, including such things as restoring city bus service, distributing food, procuring forty more coffins, and preparing for a citywide funeral on the 29th. The new Struggle Committee's seven-point resolution was read at the fifth mass rally at 3 P.M.; in the name of Kwangju's citizens, it demanded the following:

1. The Choi Kyu-ha interim government holds full responsibility for the current situation and should resign after paying full reparations to the people of Kwangju;
2. Martial law must be lifted immediately. It justifies the violence against Kwangju;
3. Execute the butcher Chun Doo Hwan in the name of the nation;
4. Release dissident leaders and form a national salvation government with them;
5. Stop the biased news coverage that distorts the uprising;
6. Our fundamental demand is not just the unconditional release of the arrested insurgents and full compensation, but a real democratic government;
7. We will fight to the death if our demands are not met (Hwang Sŏk Yŏng 1985:202–203).

At the end of the rally, the leadership announced that the military invasion could very well come that night. At 9 P.M., after a final effort to persuade the hard-liners to surrender their weapons, those young people and ordinary citizens who wanted to turn in the guns and settle the uprising left the Provincial Office Building and only those who decided to continue fighting remained (KMHRI 1990:127).

Meanwhile, in the afternoon citizens continued to file into the Sangmugwan to view the bodies. Students with microphones and white sashes to identify them guarded the entrance and directed people into seats in the balcony. Citizens waited patiently outside in a long line to attend the ten-minute memorial service. The crowd did not seem so large to me except that about five hundred people at a time could watch, it took about twenty minutes per group, and this had been going on all afternoon and also during the previous day. Mother and I had to wait about forty minutes for our turn; thousands of citizens must have come through. We looked down on fifty-three coffins on the gym floor; they brought in one more as we watched. Each was wrapped in hemp cloth, many with identifying information written on them, and most also were draped with the Korean flag. Some had pictures and memorabilia placed on top, so there was some sense of who the victims were. Here, a young student, his high school picture showing him strong and serious; there, a young woman portrayed in *hanbok* (traditional Korean dress). There were older people too; some pictures showed mature men and women. Each coffin had a pile of incense burning in front of it and offerings. Only family members were allowed on the main floor, and there were mourners around many of the coffins. Two young sisters, I supposed, were beside their brother's body, holding each other and reading a bible. A whole family stood together, a middle-aged woman weeping, arms around the casket itself. Men in hemp mourning hats sat on their haunches around the edges of the gym, quietly talking; mothers in white mourning *hanbok* leaned on each other for support. Several Buddhist monks walked about. A main altar was just visible below us, set with proper offerings.

The service started, led by a college student, his voice hoarse. A girl in high school uniform spoke, followed by a boy in fatigues, then a young man wrapped in the national flag. Remember the dead. Think of democracy. There were no wild exhortations or radical talk; the scene spoke for itself.

Watchers wept. A grandmother behind me pushed at my shoulder to get a better glimpse, and beside me Mother kept gasping, "*Omae!*" (My goodness!) as she took inventory of the victims. For the first time I really felt the dimensions of the tragedy; there before us all was the evidence that all kinds of citizens—young, old, male, female, innocent, and maybe not so innocent—had died. We sang the national anthem, and the service ended with a middle-aged, apparently middle-class man reminding us of the uncertainty of what might happen that night and of how the whole thing would end. Then we all filed out, making room for the next group.

All the way home, Mother kept dabbing at her eyes. "I can't help it," she said. "The tears just keep coming. Think of it! A young mother . . . those students . . ."

Popular Hopes Crushed

The Army Retakes the City

May 27

6:00 A.M.

At dawn—before 5 A.M.—the sound of guns. Not just the ping, ping of guns and the ak-ak-ak of automatics, but big booms that I thought might be tanks and M said was dynamite. It's a lovely day—clear, cool. F said—they must be all over the city; look on the little hill by the tracks. And sure enough, several soldiers were creeping over it. The damn helicopter sound— 5 (M says 10) circle overhead and have been for 30 minutes.

7:00

There was silence—now the helicopters are flying over broadcasting (I think), "Give up your guns." Not so much as a baby's cry in the neighbor-hood, altho I'm sure every household is like ours—out in the courtyard, washing, shaving, brushing teeth, waiting, rattling dishes. The helicopters have been flying for 30 minutes. But now—in the beautiful morning—I had assumed they would come in and take over. But I looked out and saw a guy in a house behind emerge in a yaebigun *[reservist's] uniform. I asked M— ours or theirs? Oh—it's okay. He should be out like that—he's ours. And people are appearing on kimchee pot platforms, looking around. It may be far from over. . . .*

52

8:30

The Austins say it's all over. They came in fast and big at dawn and there were few casualties. The soldiers are back in control of the city.

6:00 P.M.

Gloom in the family—except for F, who shows obvious relief and is back to his old self. TN is really shell-shocked; he can hardly talk. M is in bad shape, too. I think she has been crying. She feels for the people who have died. And we all think of all the students hauled off. Reports are 207 students arrested, 2 killed. . . . The radio is talking about rebuilding, money, etc. What is there to clean up? It is the govt buildings. And will they give compensation? M says—why should I pay taxes? What has the govt done with my money but make planes and guns to kill our students? And we have to pay 800 W a month on our TV for KBS—it is the national station, but what does it broadcast but lies? Now, is it supposed to do that? I think I'll stop paying. It is a lovely day—maybe the best of the month. Clear, so clear—and cool. We really are locked in today. They are allowing people with business (govt office types) to walk around, but only after showing IDs. There are hundreds of troops in the city, and tanks at major intersections (so I hear). No bean sprouts—M checked. They couldn't get them in, because they would have had to go by the tanks at Sansu intersection. I've slept, listened to the radio, and read Levi-Strauss today. I'm about to go stir crazy. Thorpe appeared to chat with me and the family. The family feels secure that the truth is in good hands. I sacrificed a can of soup for supper (field journal, May 27, 1980).

AT MIDNIGHT THE LONG-DISTANCE PHONE line in the Provincial Office Building had gone dead; the standoff was over. Small units of *simin'gun* were strategically deployed around the city. Of the perhaps five hundred mainly young people who had been in the headquarters during the day, only about two hundred remained, ten of them women.[1] About fifty members of the women's bureau (including some wives of the male leadership) were at the YWCA, although most eventually fled to a nearby church.

In both public and private memory, the strongest representation of that last night remains the lone voice of a young woman. Pak Yŏng-sun, a twenty-one-year-old college student, had been doing "street broadcasts" (*kadu pangsong*), a woman's job, since May 24. The street broadcasters used a makeshift sound truck to drive around the streets of Kwangju disseminating information. In the early morning hours of May 27, the final broadcast came: " Citizens! Now the martial law forces are invading! Our beloved brothers and sisters are dying from the soldiers' guns and bayonets. If we all rise up, we can defeat them. We will defend Kwangju to the end!" (cited in Hwang Sŏk Yŏng 1985:236). We all heard it, lying silently in our homes, knowing the sad truth: no matter how many thousands had thronged the fountain plaza in the bright sunlight of the previous afternoon, no one would now heed her call. No righteous army would suddenly materialize to stand against the tanks that were at that very moment rolling inexorably toward Kŭmnamno.

The military operation to retake the city began at 3:30 A.M.; by 4:00 A.M. there was a tank column in front of the Provincial Office Building, and by 5:30 A.M. the troops were mopping things up.

The activists' last stand that night was a collective action, but death came to individuals. At least twenty-six died (BFA 1989:333), mostly defending the Provincial Office Building but also at the YWCA and elsewhere, and over two hundred were taken prisoner. The military's claim that it would exercise restraint and avoid undue use of force is belied by eyewitness accounts of soldiers brutally hog-tying young men with wire and kicking them in the head and searching house to house, pulling people out of homes, shops, and inns (Warnberg 1988:46).[2]

Scant hours before the final assault, a group of foreign journalists attended a press conference held by the activist leaders. Bradley Martin writes of the then nameless spokesperson: "I was sitting directly across a coffee table from him in a room in the provincial capital building in Kwangju and I was thinking that this man would be dead soon. His eyes were directly on mine and I was thinking that he himself knew that he would be dead soon" (Martin 1997:70). Those who resolved to remain in the Provincial Office Building were prepared to fight to the death. Many, like Yun Sang-wŏn, the man Martin remembered, were killed, and others were not.

In 1996 I met one of the survivors, a man described to me as a "5.18 continuous struggle person" for his years of ongoing devotion to the cause. At the time he had been a student, newly returned to college after completing his compulsory military service; unlike other in-surgents, he was a married man with a child. I could not help asking him why he had decided to stay. His reply was quite simple: he told me that he was not concerned about how people might judge his ac-tions; rather, it was a matter of self-respect. Even though they all knew they would certainly be defeated, he understood that this was the course of all liberation movements in Korean history—the will-ingness of some to fight to the end. No one had expected the govern-ment to use such force in Kwangju, and he felt he had no choice but to continue the struggle for the honor of the uprising itself.

Another of those who survived the final assault was Kim Yŏng-ch'ŏl. Kim, thirty-two years old, married, and the father of three young children, was a political activist before 5.18; he worked with the urban poor through the YWCA credit union movement. When the new leadership was organized on May 25 as the Citizens and Stu-dents Struggle Committee, he was appointed planning director, and he was in the Provincial Office Building at dawn on May 27. In the final assault, he suffered contusions on his head and shoulders and while in detention at Sangmudae attempted suicide. Sentenced to twelve years in prison for his role in the uprising, in December 1981 his wife found him at 3 A.M., wandering outside his house, partially paralyzed and mentally deranged.[3] She struggled for several years to keep him at home, but he required constant supervision. He banged his head on the floor and walls, ran naked through the neighborhood, was caught shoplifting, and suffered from delusions. He still imagines that his comrades-in-arms from 1980 are alive and talks about meet-ing them. Finally, he had to be institutionalized (KMHRI 1990:218–224; Lee Jae-eui 1995:84).

His wife, Kim Sun-ja, has had a hard time supporting their fam-ily. In 1989, she bought a small restaurant near the Kwangju train sta-tion with the compensation money she received (Lee Jae-eui 1995:84). It is patronized by 5.18 movement members; I ate there myself in 1996 with the women of the local Min'gahyŏp chapter (a group for the families of those arrested and/or imprisoned), which holds its monthly meetings at the establishment.

On May 23, 1997, Kim Sun-ja was one of those giving personal testimony at the annual May Women's Day Memorial Service. Recount-ing how neighborhood children used to taunt her own youngsters, shouting, "Your dad's crazy!," she broke into tears, saying, "I still can't talk about this." I looked around the audience at the other women, many of whom were crying too. They must have heard this particular story many times, I thought, even more than I, yet it was still powerful.[4]

May 29

I did not write any field notes for May 29, 1980, so I cannot recheck my memory of leaving Kwangju as the most frightening experience of my life. The day before, May 28, things had eased up a bit, and it was possible to go out. I went out to look at the cleanup operation. Soldiers with shovels were cleaning up piles of trash and refuse. There were cordons around some buildings, ID checks at a few places, and still no telephone calls or bus transportation outside the city. In the afternoon I went to visit friends and also to the Kwangju District Court, where the judges were at work, but I learned it would be the next week before I could resume my research. Downtown I had met up with Don Baker, a fellow graduate student and former Peace Corps Volunteer in Kwangju, who had come down from Seoul to check on his wife's relatives. He stayed with my family that night, and the next day I decided to go along with him back to Seoul.

We set out in the late morning on Thursday, May 29. The streets were full, taxis were running, and the city bus system had just resumed operation. We took a taxi to Songjŏng-ni, at the edge of town. Others were having to get out of their taxis and walk over a bridge, through lines of troops, to get to the suburban taxis waiting on the other side, but somehow we were allowed to ride through. A tout was yelling, "To Seoul by bus for 10,000 W!"—about five times the usual price, but we hopped into his cab for the ride to the Songjŏng-ni station.

The station was packed, and we sat in a hot bus for forty-five minutes while, amid confusion and heckling from other exasperated passengers, the driver waited until the bus was full (to overflowing— a seat in the aisle went for a discounted 8,000 W).

We were actually on a local express bus (chikhaeng), supposedly destined for a nearby county. So initially we headed there through the countryside. The normal five-hour trip to Seoul took over eight hours, the first four spent on back roads to Chŏngup, where we could get on the expressway to Seoul. As we quickly learned, the highway was closed in South Chŏlla Province; getting to Seoul first involved eluding various roadblocks and military checkpoints to get out of the province.

We were stopped eight or ten times, each a slightly different experience. Soldiers would board the bus, sometimes with guns and bayonets at the ready, once only with pistols. Sometimes they were polite, but more often, surly. They asked for citizens' ID cards and inspected our faces closely. Once, all the male passengers were ordered off, with their luggage, for a thorough search. (The men immediately took the opportunity to wander off to relieve themselves, to the distress of the soldiers.) "What do you do?" they would interrogate some young man. "You visited your brother? His name? Your employer? Phone number?" The first time, some unemployed youth said that they had gone to Kwangju "to play." When the bus pulled out again, their fellow passengers advised them, "Don't say that! Say you are a farmer or a minister." At the next roadblock, one of them tried it out, replying that he was a minister. He was hauled off the bus and detained. As we went on without him, the passengers agreed he should have said he was a priest instead.

At one stop, we were ordered to turn around; a soldier got on the bus and said we had all been "taken" by the driver. Only the persistence of a white-collar worker (who outtalked the soldier) got us going again. Occasionally we were hailed by farmers standing beside the road who thought we really were a country bus heading where our sign said "This presents a problem" (*kunil natta*) muttered the bus driver, letting the people on, then dropping them off as soon as we were out of sight of soldiers and other onlookers.

Finally, we reached the expressway and picked up speed on our way to Seoul. As a suburban bus with South Chŏlla Province plates, we were rather conspicuous. Twice our bus was stopped by patrolling cops. "How much did you pay him?" came a voice from the back as we pulled away from the first such incident. We were all nervous when at 10 P.M. we approached the tollbooth just before Seoul. All vehicles were being checked, but we got special treatment. A soldier pointing a gun at all of us and saying, "Don't move!" directed the driver across several lanes of traffic. We were boarded by eight men, one in civilian clothes. People were pulled off for questioning, then allowed back on. "What is this, checkpoint eight or nine?" grumbled one passenger. From outside, a soldier replied, "You should have been checked at least fifteen times!" The stop was short but tense. When we were finally allowed on our way, everyone cheered, and one man ventured the opinion, "At 10,000 W, this was cheap!"

They unloaded us in a hurry in front of the new express bus terminal in Kangnam at 10:15 P.M., less than two hours before curfew. As a country bus with the wrong markings, the best the driver could do was pull in with a lot of city buses and hope no one would notice. At that time, the bus terminal was in the middle of nowhere, and even getting a taxi was a problem. I went to a telephone booth and starting calling friends to see who could put me up for the night.

"Kwangju Continues"

The Summer of 1980 and Beyond

The Immediate Aftermath

*Two days back [from a trip to Seoul and Tokyo] and it feels oppressive
again. . . . I met [my friend] at a tearoom, took her her gifts. She was willing
to talk a lot. It is true—less tension here than in Seoul, and people remain
open, unafraid. Why? She says the govt is afraid to do anything down here.
They try to put soldiers on every corner, and the place will blow up again. So
maybe this is the safest place to be. We discussed paranoia—ah, yes. A little
gum seller hung around; [my friend] sent him away "Sometimes the govt
sends kids around to report on conversations." She also is afraid of an anti-
Amer wave, brought on by/fomented by govt lies. Is it over? is it just beginning? Is it in the middle? I think I [should] decide it is over and get back to
work (field journal, June 8, 1980).*

BUT I WAS WRONG; the Kwangju Uprising was far from over. The collective nightmare of May was followed by the shared emotional devastation of the summer and fall of 1980. The rest of that year was a
particularly tense, uncertain, and depressing period in all of South Korea, but life was especially bleak and full of sorrow in Kwangju. In
April Chun Doo Hwan had illegally made himself director of the Korean Central Intelligence Agency (KCIA), the country's most powerful
civilian organization. Throughout the summer he maneuvered cro-
nies into key positions, and in August he succeeded Choi Kyu-ha as

interim president. In October a new constitution was drawn up and submitted to a rubber-stamp national referendum: the corrupt and oppressive Fifth Republic had formally begun. In February 1981 an electoral college under ruling party control elected the now civilian Chun to a single, seven-year term as president (see Eckert et al. 1990: 372–375). In Seoul, Kim Dae Jung (with twenty-three codefendants) was put on trial and sentenced to death for sedition, Communist ties, and violations of the National Security Law in connection with 5.18;[1] in Kwangju, people kept being hunted down over the summer, detained, interrogated, often tortured, and convicted in a secret military court for their part in the May uprising.

"When will we all find a new topic of conversation," I wondered on June 11 (field journal); my field notes, until I left Kwangju on October 10, daily record some sort of political conversation—tidbits exchanged, gossip, rumors, speculation, heated discussions, and always memories of May.

It was dangerous to publicly discuss 5.18. On June 23 I first heard (from Mother) the apocryphal tale of a man from Kwangju who got into a taxi in Seoul. The driver asked about the Kwangju "incident," so the passenger told him what had happened—at which point the driver went straight to the military police and had the passenger arrested for spreading false rumors. Years later, that story was still being told, but real cases (noted in my journal) were all too frequent: reporters fired for writing that the paratroopers had killed people; university students arrested for distributing pamphlets about the uprising; and doctors afraid to show pictures they had taken of victims revealing their wounds. Still, the conversations went on; after dinner one evening with an elderly lawyer and his friend from Mokp'o, I wrote that they "discussed events in hushed tones . . . —sympathies with Kwangju, of course ('One man [that is, Chun] is doing it all'). And like other people they say, 'Be careful,' then proceed to talk. We didn't say much in the restaurant, but even on the street, remarks are made. He talked about how tight things were in Seoul. Truly, people down here aren't afraid, and the atmosphere is better. There is a lot of civic pride going around" (field journal, June 8, 1980). The atmosphere in Kwangju lacked the sense of foreboding that seemed to hang over the rest of the country; perhaps in Honam people felt they had already gone through the worst that could happen.

Friends shared experiences and sought solace in the telling of their stories. At the courthouse, everyone claimed he or she had been downtown at the Provincial Office Building plaza each day. A judge wept as he recalled witnessing troops fire into crowds of demonstrators near Chŏnnam University. One day as I was coming back from lunch with several judges, our taxi stopped at a traffic light behind a truck. As the truck started up, it backfired loudly, and all of us jumped. After a moment of shocked silence, we all began to talk about how we were now easily frightened by loud noises and the sound of helicopters.

Perhaps because of the inability of Kwangju's citizens to construct a public, national narrative of 5.18, the story was told and retold instead within small groups, as people sought mutual comfort within the community itself. This served to consolidate and reinforce the feeling of regional isolation and victimization within Kwangju and the larger Honam area and encouraged the region's citizens to find a shared meaning in the event itself that stressed those elements. It would not be until the 1990s that competing narratives could begin publicly to emerge.

Within my own household, the uprising also lived on. On June 16, for example, it was "the usual political discussion at dinner. The govt is now actively looking for a large number of students and profs. We really have the spectrum here. M represents the common man's view—from the gut, non-ideological, but with honest, truthful emotion. Let's call it what it is, is what she figures. TN is the youthful idealist. And F is the cautious self-protector. I am amazed at the amount of political dialogue. And the freeness of it. M yells at F—in fact, they both do, in asking him how he can allow himself to be fooled. Do all households discuss politics (field journal)?"

The debates included even the extended family. When Mother's parents were visiting, political discussions raged in the courtyard, with Father and Grandfather constantly arguing. When the government announced in late July that it would put Kim Dae Jung on trial and seek the death penalty, Mother went about her household chores in sullen silence, forbidden by Father to speak about the issue.

Citizens, especially in Kwangju, were mobilized in public displays of support for Chun, and those who through their jobs were vulnerable to political pressure were constantly called upon to demonstrate their loyalty. My artist friend, a professor at Chosŏn University, was distressed when a group of several hundred professors and students were forced to go on a weekend trip to view the North Korean tunnels under the DMZ; it would, Tong-nip predicted, be reported in the newspapers as a group who begged to be taken there. Professors were also being harassed about their students. My friend was particularly upset in September when people from the government started coming around her department at the university looking for a student who had been politically active. Staff members warned the student to stay away, but apparently in other cases professors and staff were complicit in apprehending students.

Even Father's willingness to go stoically along with the new regime flagged as the summer wore on. Father's moment of reckoning came when, as a civil servant, he was spending long days in the countryside holding meetings and distributing government propaganda in an effort to ensure passage of the new constitution:

> *I came home to hear Father relate how today they had been at a meeting about the Referendum. They have been given stuff to pass out; they have to go forth and brainwash. And there are checks in the system, so that people have to give proof that they actually have conducted these training sessions, etc. He was really disgusted (M more so—she was really swearing). But F says what they do is the minimum in form. They go out, then come back to report that they went. Out there, they say—okay, you all come vote. And the villagers say—okay. All form, no content. Giving it their least, one might say. Doesn't show much in the way of guts, but it may keep your job (field journal, September 25, 1980).*

Meanwhile, people kept disappearing, making a cruel joke of the martial law authorities' assurances in May that there would be no reprisals. In June, hundreds of people were being sought, many with large bounties on their heads, and everyone, it seemed (even me), knew someone in jail. The number of academics taken in for questioning, even in Seoul, grew, a point that was underscored in late July, when Valerie Steenson, the new director of the ACC in Kwangju, tried to organize a dinner party to meet "friends" (largely professors and civic leaders) of the ACC. She kept having to alter the guest list as her invitees were, one by one, taken into detention; finally, she was forced to cancel the party altogether when there were not enough people still free to come (field journal, July 24–31, 1980).

Several thousand people were arrested in connection with 5.18, over 600 of whom were detained. The charges against 212 were dropped, but 404 citizens eventually stood trial in military court and about 200 were convicted and sentenced in October 1980 (Clark, ed. 1988:91), 5 to death, 7 to life in prison, and many others to heavy jail terms. In December 1980 an appellate court upheld about 100 of the earlier convictions, including 3 of the death sentences (Communiqué, July 4, 1981, p. 49). On March 30, 1981, the Supreme Court ruled on the cases, also upholding many of the lower court rulings, but in April, in response to widespread domestic and international appeals, the Chun government reduced the sentences of 83 defendants (Communiqué, May 10, 1981, p. 23).

The trials were conducted in near total secrecy at Sangmudae; journalists and international observers were denied access, and even attendance by family members of the defendants was strictly limited. Prayer vigils were held outside the army base gates, but information about what was going on inside was largely rumor and speculation.

Because I was at the time interviewing lawyers in the course of my dissertation research, I was able to learn something about the defendants' lack of adequate counsel:

> *I was really surprised when XXX walked in, because he is the least likely candidate for one of the most successful lawyers in town—his suits always bag at the seat, his face is red, and his eyes rummy; he looks like a tortoise in motion. But you forget all that when you talk to him. Sharp, but patient. Helpful. I liked him a lot. And—lots of info. Esp on the military court. Normally the court-appointed defense lawyer serves right at the district court, so sticks with the case. But the [court-appointed defense lawyers at the military trials] are "special" in that [the hearings] run every day. That means no lawyer can be expected to drop all his other cases to be out there day after day. So the lawyers' association has set up a rotation—2 a day go out. They expect all [Kwangju's lawyers] will go 3 times. They think that the cases are being taken light to heavy, and no one is really sure how much longer they will go—[XXX's] next date isn't set. He thinks he defended about 20 ordinary citizens. He didn't speak to his clients, didn't know who they were or what the cases were before he went, had only the prosecution brief to look at. Then he had to "intuit" the nature of the case and improvise a defense on the spot, listening to the judge's questions. There was little a lawyer could*

do—most were open and closed. —"Did you participate in the demo?" —
"Yes." What can a lawyer do? He says he really doesn't know much about
the contents of the cases he defended that day. Each person can have 1 or 2
family members in the courtroom. Each person could also hire their own
lawyer, or two. But most haven't (he thinks maybe a defendant or two has a
lawyer, but he isn't sure). Why? Well, first, it is hopeless—the charges are
clear and it is assumed even the best defense won't help. How can they pre-
pare a defense? They can't even talk to the defendants. Normally, relatives
talk to the defendants and hire a lawyer on the basis of what they know of
the case. But here, where no one is even sure of the charges. . . . Plus—will
they get paid? Plus—how to work this in with the regular court schedule (im-
possible). Plus—appeals will be heard in Seoul and who can go there?? So—
all in all. . . . It turns my stomach (field journal, September 27, 1980).[2]

Stories about the situations of those in custody circulated. A
friend confided that the families of some professors were doing all
right, but he was worried about the wife and children of one man; he
had heard the wife had opened a noodle shop to support herself but
that the business was not doing well. A college student told me about
a second-year high school student she knew arrested for organizing
other students. She had had to bribe a guard 10,000 W to visit him in
prison. In early August, the boy was released, but my friend reported
he was listless and apathetic, suffered from chronic head and stomach
aches, and, as a result of not bathing, had a skin rash.

Prison joined together odd cellmates. Hong Kŭm-suk, the teen-
ager who survived the minibus massacre, recalled that at first she had
been in solitary confinement but later was kept together with others,
including Cho A-ra, the elderly head of the YWCA (KMHRI 1990:
971). The jails were also overcrowded. The "5.18 Sacred Places Pilgrimage" pamphlet describes Sangmudae:

As the Chŏlla Do martial law headquarters, this was where those
taken into custody were held and tortured and assaulted and
confined, and it was also the place where the courtroom was, where
the military trials of the citizens' militia members were conducted.

The jail at this place, a brick and slate-roofed structure, at the
time of 5.18 held 150, in a cell designed to accommodate 30 prisoners, and so a meal for 30 was divided and eaten by 150 people. We can

imagine the misery of those detained here, who suffered mistreatment from hunger, and the steam-cooker heat.

Also, right beside the jail was the courthouse in which the military trials were being held (AEC 1995).

Later, material published by human rights groups in Japan provided more explicit and detailed information on those in custody and the conditions of their arrest and confinement. In particular, Kwangju defendants were tortured and forced to sign "confessions" implicating Kim Dae Jung as the government worked to fabricate its case against the popular opposition politician.[3] A January 1981 "Statement from the Families of the Kwangju Trial Defendants" charged that "As if they had a 'Kim Dae Jung complex,' the detectives tried without any basis in fact to connect all the prisoners to Kim Dae Jung. Their questions included the following: 'Do you respect Kim Dae Jung?'; 'Do you want him to become president?'; and 'If he had become president, what did he promise to offer you for your support?'" (Commmuniqué, July 4, 1981, p. 48). One example was the sixty-eight-year-old lawyer, Hong Nam-sun, who was part of the Namdong church group and who received a sentence of life imprisonment at his first trial. As the families' "Statement" noted,

> Mr. Hong was urged to join the Kwangju citizens' control committee by Mr. Chung Yong-tae, then an intelligence officer in the Kwangju City Police Force; Mr. Chung Shi-chae, the vice governor of Chunnam Province; and Mr. Chung Chae-kyun, the vice mayor of Kwangju City.
>
> Lawyer Hong was deprived of sleep during 38 days of investigation. Meanwhile, his wife and one of his sons were held in prison as hostages.[4] His clerk, Chung Kwang-jin, was arrested and released only after 68 days. His oldest son, his brother-in-law, and a niece were also arrested. Such was the extreme mental torture Mr. Hong had to endure, leading him to make a false confession to the effect that he had received 20 million Won from Mr. Kim Dae-jung in order to stage demonstrations at both Chunnam and Chosŏn Universities (Communiqué, July 4, 1981, pp. 48–49).

The torture inflicted on the 5.18 detainees was not only mental, but physical as well. A December 10, 1980, letter from the families of those in

custody to the Catholic cardinal in Seoul cited many cases; among them
was that of Kim Chong-bae, a twenty-nine-year-old student:

> Mr. Kim was detained at dawn on the 27th of May by the Martial Law
> Command for having held the position of student representative on the
> Citizens' Committee to Seek Solutions to the Kwangju Disturbance. He
> was tortured day and night, was hit on the head with an M-16 rifle butt,
> had two teeth broken, was beaten severely on the face and forehead,
> and still bears the scars from all of these beatings. Only after losing con-
> sciousness three times and having been subjected to forms of violence
> and torture beyond human imagination did he bend to his interroga-
> tors' demands that he put his fingerprint on the false "confession" con-
> tained in the indictment (Communiqué, March 1, 1981, p. 40).

Also the case of Park Yon-son, another university student:

> At the urging of his father, Mr. Park turned himself in to the Joint In-
> vestigative Command on June 3. From that time until June 7, he was
> beaten and tortured repeatedly, and on suffering severe damage to his
> spinal cord, he fell into a coma. Even after he was transferred to the
> army's General Hospital in Kwangju and although he showed signs of
> mental disorder, he was not given appropriate treatment. Instead, he
> was made to take painkillers continuously and has lost his ability to
> speak. The indictment against him has been terminated for the
> present, yet his family's request to have him released due to his severe
> physical ailment was refused. He is still being held in the intensive
> care ward of the hospital (Communiqué, March 1, 1981, p. 40).

Many of the very people who out of concern over further bloodshed had joined in the Incident Settlement Committee and who had
worked to persuade the *simin'gun* to turn in their weapons were now
charged with being "central figures in a national insurrection." One
of them, Father Kim Sŏng-yong, who at the time was assigned to the
Namdong church in Kwangju, spoke to this point at his trial in his
final statement to the court on October 23, 1980:

> What will happen to a country which arraigns Catholic clergy on
> charges of plotting insurrection? A country which labels as insurgents

the priests who acted to bring things under control when the incidents occurred cannot last long and I feel no hope for this country. I have no desire to live any longer if it must be in a country like this. We were arrested and indicted on charges of inciting insurrection and we underwent trial for those alleged crimes. But what about the person who destroyed the interim government of President Choi Kyu-ha . . . [the magistrate stops Father Kim here, threatening to remove him from the court if he makes any disparaging remarks about the former or present head of state] (cited in Commmuniqué, May 10, 1981, p. 22).

The start of the trials brought a few reporters back to Kwangju; on October 10 I noted that CNN reporter Mike Chinoy was in town covering demonstrations by Catholic activists outside the army base. In fact I saw a rather constant flow of visitors to Kwangju throughout the summer and early fall: journalists, human rights activists, representatives of church groups, Korean specialists, assorted friends, and even a professor of mine from Columbia University—all, in one way or another, with their own agendas concerning 5.18. Martha Huntley recalled that "A large number of groups—mostly Christian—came in a steady stream to investigate what had happened in Kwangju and how another such tragedy could be prevented. We helped them with housing, food, and translation" (1982:14).

Like the Huntleys, most of us in the foreign community who had been in Kwangju in May felt an obligation to bear witness to what we had seen and to what we knew had happened. We cared that the truth of the "Kwangju Sat'ae" (Kwangju Incident) should be told. Yet many of those who made the pilgrimage to Kwangju that summer came with their own ideas about the meaning of 5.18 and already knew what they wanted to hear; entertaining them was often a frustrating experience. "I'm tired of finding things out [for people], then being treated like the information wasn't important," I wrote on October 10 (field journal). I learned that when people did not like the news (for example, the fact that in general Kwangju citizens felt the U.S. government was supporting Chun) or thought the answer too equivocal (for example, death estimates varied widely), they tended to dismiss the informant. The problem was particularly acute with reporters and with anyone connected with the U.S. government. On October 2, I stopped by the ACC to pick up my mail and found that

Val [the Center director] was feeling really blue—she had had some bigwigs [US Embassy officials] down the day before from Seoul. She had some [Korean] staff over for dinner, and the bigwigs said—so what do people down here think? At which point, they got honest answers. Of course, all the Kwangjuites were accused of being emotional, too involved, etc. Val was quite disillusioned. Well, welcome to the club—it is hard being from here. People pump you, then when they don't agree, make you feel like shit. She should have been here through the incident; then she'd really know what it felt like to be an overwrought, unobjective source. Of course, embassy personnel are beyond belief. . . . I wonder if the people in Iran [in the US Embassy] were as deserving candidates for their fate as the people here would be, should a similar event take place (field journal).

If my identification with Kwangju was a difficulty in dealing with outsiders, I found my position as a U.S. citizen to be equally problematic in continuing to live there myself. In retrospect, 1980 marks the beginning of anti-Americanism in South Korea.[5] Indeed, some of my friends expressed anxiety about the rising tide of anti-American sentiment. Still, I did not take their concerns too seriously. It is a truism that anti-Americanism in South Korea manifests itself at the ideological level, in impassioned rhetoric and symbolic displays, rather than at an interpersonal level, in threats to the safety of individual Americans. I never felt it was physically dangerous to remain in Kwangju; rather, the distress I experienced was emotional. I was constantly confronted that summer about my government's actions, subjected to tirades about what America should (or should not) do or had (or had not) done, and forced to endure endless harangues about U.S. foreign policy. Strangers felt compelled to stop me on the street and try to engage me in political debate. On July 5, noting that living in Kwangju was becoming excessively depressing, I wrote that "I hope something will happen. Deep down inside, I know it won't, because people will just go on about their business. It is like something out of fantasyland—tomorrow they will arrest someone for saying the sky is blue. The other side is—I have already had two [such] conversations— the US could save Kim for us if they wanted to. To hell with this place" (field journal).

As it happened, the United States could "save" Kim Dae Jung. On February 2, 1981, Chun Doo Hwan had the honor of being the first head of state to visit the Reagan White House, but before his visit to Washington, Chun ended martial law, announced an amnesty for political prisoners, and commuted Kim's death sentence to life in prison (see Cohen and Baker 1991:195–196).

Counting the Cost

How many people died in the Kwangju Uprising? In 1980, when I was asked that question and could not give with certainty a precise number, people would turn away from me impatiently, as if I had failed some credibility test. But I wondered why it was important to know exactly how many were killed. Is there some magic figure that makes a difference—as if 189 dead is fine, but 190 victims would be unacceptable? To know the stories of Kim Kyŏng-ch'ŏl, Kim Pong-man, Kim Myŏng-ch'ŏl, Ch'oe Mi-ae, Kim Chae-p'yŏng, Kim Ch'un-nye, and Pang Kwang-bŏm should be enough; how many more would one need to conclude that something terrible had happened in Kwangju?

Those days in the early summer of 1980, with the government acknowledging only a few deaths and the Incident Settlement Committee estimating almost 1,500 (KCS 1997:153), are long since past. The official government death toll (in 1997) is 238; that figure includes 191 known fatalities (164 civilians, 23 soldiers, and 4 police officers) (Clark, ed. 1988:91), as well as 47 of the missing who have been officially classified as victims. Responsible estimates in Kwangju now would put the figure up to only about 200 more, or between 400 and 500 victims.

There are several reasons why groups in Kwangju still claim slightly higher numbers. The most obvious have to do with petitions by families of those missing during the uprising and presumed dead. Although almost fifty claims have been accepted (after an investigation process that included review by a committee made up in part of Kwangju citizens), over one hundred more have not. In over two-thirds of the missing persons' registered cases, then, there has not been sufficient evidence to prove conclusively that the person was a 5.18 casualty; the families of course believe their loved ones must have been killed at that time. Many people in Kwangju are also convinced the army secretly buried bodies (*ammaejang*), a suspicion kept alive by the continuing occasional discovery of bodies, rumors about the location of grave sites, and the relatively large number of those still unaccounted for. It is in fact a common assumption that the number of missing is actually higher even than the number of registered claims. After all, to be claimed as missing requires a family to notice one's disappearance. Many suspect that some of those killed and dumped in unknown graves in May 1980 were juvenile delinquents, homeless youth, and unemployed young men—just the sort of people who would be swept up in the street violence and then never missed.

There are also different ways of calculating the human cost of 5.18. When I asked the head of the Injured People's Association, Pak Yŏng-sun, in 1996 for statistics on the victims, the figures he gave me included 2,710 injured and 284 dead (154 citizens who died at the time, 83 who had died since, and 47 missing). The Bereaved Families' Association for Those Who Died after 5.18 (5.18 Sangihu Samangja Yujokhoe) lists 154 (civilian) deaths at the time, 12 victims whose exact date of death is unknown, and 120 who have died since May 27, 1980.[6] These counts do not include the noncivilian deaths. If those and also the missing are added, the number of known deaths comes to well over 300.

Eight people died of their 5.18-related injuries between May 27, 1980, and the end of that year; fourteen more died in 1981. Four people died in the first half of 1997—are they part of the Kwangju Uprising body count? The lives of many of the injured will be foreshortened as a result; they also are more prone to such problems as alcoholism, drug addiction (for pain), and psychological disorders (Byun 1996). What about Chang Pok-sun, who was injured by a blow to her head and was in and out of mental hospitals until she finally committed suicide in 1993 (Lee Jae-eui 1995:94.) Is she a 5.18 "fatality"? Family members of those who died are also at risk; Kim Chŏm-sul, a farmer, drank himself to death three years after his fifty-year-old wife, Pak Yŏn-ok, was killed by paratroopers (BFA 1989:275; Lee Jae-eui. 1995:95). Is his death part of the statistics?

In May 2000, I stood on the upper tier at the May 18 Cemetery in Kwangju beside the new grave of Myŏng No-gŭn with his widow, city councilwoman Ahn Sung-ryae. Myŏng, an English professor at Chŏnnam University, had been a supporter of the students' committee inside the Provincial Office Building in 1980; I had interviewed him in 1997, when he was chairman of the Seventeenth Anniversary

Events Committee. He was sixty-six years old when he died; was his death, I asked Ahn, specifically 5.18 related? Her reply (and that of others to whom I put the same question) was simply that May victims seemed, in general, to die too soon.

In the vast, circular Photographic Memorial Hall (Yuyŏng Pongan So) of the May 18 Cemetery the portraits of the 5.18 victims, displayed in front of the altar, seem to take up a fraction of the available space; to the right, those of the official missing victims occupy an even smaller part of it. It took me a while to realize that the rest of the room was intended to house the pictures of those injured in 5.18, who, one by one, as they die, can be buried in the May 18 Cemetery. Perhaps when the Photographic Memorial Hall is full, the human cost of the Kwangju Uprising will be clearer.

PART II

City of Light/
City of Outlaws

Truth Telling in
the Fifth Republic

DURING THE FIFTH REPUBLIC—that is, the presidency of Chun Doo Hwan (1981–1988)—it was difficult even to speak of the Kwangju Uprising, let alone do research or attempt to write about what had happened. Lee Jae-eui tells of his apprehensions and fears as he and a few friends in 1985 began work on their definitive account, *Beyond Death, Beyond the Darkness of the Age;* they covered the windows at night so no one could see in and arranged secret signals with their families should the authorities be watching.[1]

While in a retrospective gaze these precautions seem almost quaintly cloak-and-dagger, Lee's concerns were very real. As he says, "Any publication criticizing the Chun Doo-hwan regime was completely banned. Of course, 'the truth about the Kwangju uprising' was told in an incomplete and distorted way. Given the conditions, documenting the uprising was like belling a cat" (Lee Jae-eui 1999:12). Indeed, in May 1985 the publishing house where Lee's volume was being printed was raided, copies of the unbound book were seized, and both the publisher and the "cover author" (Hwang Sŏk Yŏng) were arrested; it was not until 1987 that the book could be openly sold (Lee Jae-eui 1999:14).

Information about the Kwangju Uprising circulated underground, but harassment of publishers and print shops; raids on bookstores; and confiscation of videos, books, and other "subversive" materials found at such places as churches and the offices of student and activist groups were commonplace through much of the 1980s.[2] In fact, restrictions on the press and the suppression of free speech were (remarkably) even more severe under Chun Doo Hwan than under his predecessor.[3] As one report on human rights noted, "Were the press free, President Chun's policies, practices, and indeed his very authority would no doubt come under close scrutiny, and political opponents would be able to get their message to voters. To have a free press would be to invite political competition. This is something the South Korean government is not willing to permit" (International League For Human Rights 1985:49).

An incomplete, yet still deep and fearful, silence surrounded the "incident" of May 1980 and its larger implications. Even outside Korea it was difficult in the 1980s to get the scholarly community to confront the Kwangju issue and to discuss it openly. Nowadays I often characterize 5.18 as "Tienanmen before CNN and the fax"; the comparison is painfully apt in the sense that although there were indeed many political analysts, academics, and "friends" of Korea concerned at the time about human rights abuses under Chun, in the absence of "reliable" accounts, there were others who simply found it more convenient to believe the government's version of events in Kwangju.

In addition to willful ignorance, attempts to think, write, and talk about Kwangju were at the time constrained by the parameters of acceptable discourse and limited by fragmentary and incomplete knowledge of the event itself. As Donald Clark wrote in 1988 in the introduction to what was (and still is) one of the few works on 5.18 in English,

> If Kwangju refuted the claim to legitimacy of Chun Doo Hwan's regime, we need to know more about what really happened there. Koreans are not free to discuss the uprising and the government exhorts them to put it in the past. Yet campus demonstrations usually refer to it and have succeeded in keeping the memory of it alive. A key demand of the students who seized the United States Information Service building in Seoul in May 1985 was that there be a public hearing on Kwangju. . . . Public curiosity was such in the summer of 1985 that the government was obliged to give a public accounting of the

Kwangju incident to the National Assembly. The issue simply will not go away (Clark, ed. 1988:6).

Unfortunately, the government's report in the twelfth National Assembly session was not the "truth telling" the public was demanding. Although the return of Kim Dae Jung from exile in the United States in early 1985 and his party's subsequent success in the parliamentary elections of February 1985 broke the taboo on public discussion of the "Kwangju Incident" and Kwangju became the subject of continuous activity and debate in the National Assembly that spring, the government was resistant. The National Defense Ministry's official report of June 7, 1985, differed little from earlier accountings in June 1980 (*Kwangju ilbo*, June 1, 1985),[4] and a serious investigation of the military's role in the "Kwangju Massacre" would not be possible until the "Liquidation of the Fifth Republic" hearings in 1988.[5]

lies in the 1985 report

The 1985 official report, far from acknowledging the violence and brutality of the martial law troops (as those in Kwangju would have hoped), instead praised the restraint of the soldiers. According to the government's account, troops were called in only when on Sunday, May 18, local police were unable to maintain order (as cited in Clark, ed. 1988:84); on that day, "Young soldiers, carrying out their duty in military turmoil, had to arrest student demonstrators while citizens were watching. It was a situation in which there were more or less fierce clashes" (Clark, ed. 1988: 85).

The 1985 report goes on to detail the "reckless activities" of "wayward rioters" and "mobsters" in the early stages of the uprising but makes no mention of the troops firing on crowds of unarmed civilians. It states that "In the face of the anarchy created by armed rioters, the military refrained from exercising the right of self-defense for fear that citizens might be hurt. Even when soldiers were taken and killed by mobs, the military devoted itself to preventing a worse situation." The troops withdrew from the city on May 21 "lest their continued confrontation with rioters should incite citizens" (Clark, ed. 1988: 89). The decision to retake the city was made when "on the sixth day of the commotion, good citizens began to show signs of calming down, and it became possible to distinguish armed rioters from good citizens." The government did not believe the people could "restore order for themselves"; in addition, "As a result of the protracted anarchy, there

was an increasing possibility that impure elements or armed North Korean commandos might infiltrate Kwangju." Thus the military returned "[on] May 27, 1980, to save the citizens from anarchy" (Clark,
ed. 1988: 90).

The real cause of the uprising (from the government's perspective) was "that some political forces pulled a string for the flare-up of
the Kwangju incident."[6] "Innocent citizens" were duped into participation: "Groundless rumors fabricated by impure elements deepened
regional acrimony, set apart civilians and troops and led to arson, destruction, killings, and injuries" (Clark, ed. 1988:84). The whole tragic
episode was "a planned act by impure elements who intended to encourage the internal division and disturbance into a forceful riot" (p. 85),
and it was brought to a close only when "ordinary citizens," losing
sympathy for the "rioters," "began to feel threatened and started to return to their senses" (p. 88).

Finally, the official 1985 account portrayed Kwangju as "a city of
terror, as arson and other crimes were committed everywhere" (Clark,
ed. 1988:86), a place with armed demonstrators turning it "to a state of
lawlessness and anarchy as the city's administrative functions were
paralyzed" (p. 84). The report alleges that "some of the rioters committed murder and robberies out of personal grudges" (p. 88), that private
businesses were burned and looted (p. 87), and that the rebels "created
an atmosphere of terror in which citizens were forced to wage protracted warfare" (p. 90).

Given this official reckoning of events, alternative scholarly accounts at the time necessarily started from a defensive position as attempts to refute government narratives of 5.18 and to offer different
"truth claims" for the Kwangju Uprising. For me—someone whose
daily ethnographic field notes from May 1980 recorded a very different
reality from the image of a city full of terror-stricken citizens haplessly
caught in a state of extended mob rule—it was important to bear witness to 5.18. People in Kwangju were not innocent "dupes," the uprising was not a planned act instigated by "impure elements," and the
soldiers surely did not act with restraint. Yet in the early 1980s, in the
absence of open discussion and the possibility of research, moving beyond personal accounts of "what I saw at the revolution," to the
construction of an authoritative victim-centered narrative was problematic. Information was fragmentary, and corroboration difficult.

In writing about Kwangju, I was particularly concerned with asserting the "popular" nature of the event and with presenting alternative explanations of citizens' motivations and behavior. In 1987 in "The 'Kwangju Incident' Observed: An Anthropological Perspective on Civil Uprisings" (Lewis 1988a),[7] I began my own analysis of the meaning of 5.18 with the question posed in my field notes for May 19, 1980, about the tragedy unfolding on the city's streets:

"It is really horrible, and people can't believe it is happening and can't imagine why."

Why, indeed? Seven years later the question remains unanswered. What sense can be made of the Kwangju uprising? What meaning, or meanings, can be found in it? With the benefit now of some years' hindsight, what is the event's significance, and what implications does it hold? . . .

I would like to offer here two approaches to the Kwangju material, two perspectives of the short-run through which to make anthropological sense of the event. The first, a micro-sociological view, pays less attention to the broad political context and focuses instead on breaking down the mass of urban rebels into different groups, to distinguish between real populations, and to examine more closely the nature of popular participation in terms of who was involved, to what degree, and with what stakes in the outcome. The other approach looks at the uprising as a violent situation and is concerned with the process of rationalization on the part of the victims. What meanings did people find in the event? What assessments were made by the citizens themselves, and how did they understand, both immediately and in retrospect, the violence that took place? . . .

One of the most important points to be made about the Kwangju uprising is its "popular" nature. It was my observation that the participation in the event was city wide and involved a majority of the citizenry.[8] . . . [But] beyond the general engagement of a broad spectrum of the population, three main categories of participants in the uprising can be distinguished on the basis of the nature, extent, and timing of involvement, and stake in the outcome.

There were some groups who were mobilized on the basis of preexisting ties, and in accord with previously established (and socially recognized) channels of action and modes of public protest. These groups by and large were also involved in active opposition to government policy, particularly the imposition of martial law prior to May 18, 1980. The most obvious of these were the university students. Students in Korea have a long tradition of demonstrating against the government and are recognized as legitimate and proper leaders of public expressions of political protest.[9] Other groups in this category were members and leaders of church and other civic organizations (e.g. the YWCA and the YMCA) active in regular and continuing political opposition. It was these groups that provided leadership for the rebellion.

However, the majority of the demonstrators—by far the largest category numerically and most of the reportedly tens of thousands who demonstrated in the streets during the uprising's first days, and most of whom were not armed and would not have wanted to get hurt—were recruited individually and were not participating through channels of previously experienced collective action. Many of these people were initially engaged in the uprising in the context of neighborhood street fighting, through either witnessing some violent incident themselves or hearing a firsthand account of it. But what is significant about this majority category—the masses of the rebellion—is that they were not engaged along pre-existing lines, including class affiliation.

Finally, there were those initially constrained from acting on the basis of a common vested interest in not being labeled as participants. In this category are those, primarily government employees (judges, civil servants, school administrators—mostly men in positions of public trust) who were afraid of losing their jobs. It was not that these people disagreed with the grievances and goals of the rebellion or that they hoped the rebellion would collapse, or even that they feared for their lives. Rather . . . when the inevitable end to the uprising came and the government regained control, if they were known to have demonstrated, their positions would be in jeopardy.[10] These people were the last to show their support publicly for the uprising.

These categories of participants were engaged in the rebellion in successive stages. The event began as a student demonstration against the imposition of martial law and developed into a series of street demonstrations (in Kwangju, relatively peaceful ones) that were part of an ongoing national pattern of student demonstrations begun in early

May. There had been massive demonstrations in Seoul the previous week, and it does not seem that the students in Kwangju were in general doing anything distinctive, compared with students in other cities—except that they agreed to continue demonstrating on May 18.[11]

The situation became an uprising in a second stage, with the subsequent engagement of the largest category, the general citizenry, on May 19, 20, and 21. Initially, and as an explanation of what provoked most of the street fighting in the first days, ordinary people took to the streets as an expression of popular outrage at the brutality of government troops in suppressing the student demonstrations. It was difficult in fact to totally avoid involvement in those early days because so much street fighting went on. People went out to look, and got caught up in it, or went out to join in. There was also a significant number of people who were aware of the brutality and were outraged, but who did not venture far into the streets for fear of getting hurt. These people, however, participated in other ways (giving food, money) and demonstrated to the extent that it was not, or as soon as it ceased to be, physically dangerous.

This second stage, of engaged mass participation, was followed on May 23 by a third stage, after the troops left the center of the city, when non-violent demonstrations (in the form of mass rallies) numerically reached their peak. And this third stage was distinguished by the emergence of a new grievance, that served to involve the rest of the demonstrators (the category of initially reluctant participants), and which explains what kept people in the streets and strengthened the sense of resistance within the city, prolonging the rebellion. Without this second grievance, the uprising might have collapsed after a couple of days of street fighting. And that grievance was (and still is) that the government refused to apologize or in any way to accept responsibility for provoking the initial violence. . . .

Individual rebellions, suggests Elizabeth Perry (1980:252), combine elements of "blind accident and human will." Perhaps what made Kwangju different—in a season of violent urban protest in Korea—was that the blind accident of paratrooper brutality was combined with sufficient human will, in the form of opposition to the implementation of martial law and the return to military rule (and thus the turn away from democratic reform). The collapse of the rebellion in the face of the government's armed reentry into the city on May 27 should be viewed not as a sign of a failure of leadership or weakness of popular support so much as a realistic assessment of the lengths to which the government was willing to go in using force to suppress the rebellion. I think we have to see the Kwangju uprising as more than an example of collective violence gone out of control. . . .

It is especially significant that:

1) it was not limited to a specific segment of society (e.g. urban laborers), but involved a broad cross-section of the citizenry;

2) it did not involve the destruction of private property, and the violence on the part of the rebels to both person and property was limited to specific government-related targets;

3) it possessed a leadership that was, certainly in terms of the students, part of a national movement recognized as a force capable of transforming society; and—while the uprising itself was sparked by two specific and immediate grievances: the brutality of the government in suppressing the demonstrations and the subsequent failure of the government to accept responsibility for its actions—the more abstract political goal of the establishment of a democratic government was already in place (Lewis 1988a:16–21).

It is difficult to remember, looking back after two decades, that the labeling of 5.18 was in the mid-1980s a contested issue. Although (as we shall see in Part III) at the turn of the century the government's preferred appellation, the "5.18 Democratization Movement" (5.18 Minjuhwa Undong), drains the blood from the event, the term does recognize 5.18 as a mass political action rather than a mere riot. People in Kwangju in the late 1990s still preferred the more militant, oppositional "5.18 People's Uprising" (5.18 Minjung Hangjaeng), with its *minjung* movement overtones, yet the continued use of this name was no longer self-consciously counterhegemonic. In English translation, "the Kwangju Uprising" has long been acceptable. Yet in the 1980s, calling it that—in any language— was a political statement. The euphemistic "Kwangju Incident" was the label commonly employed by both the government and the opposition to neatly sidestep the controversy surrounding the event's essential nature, and, in the 1980s its revolutionary character was a matter still to be proven rather than presumed.

In addition to examining popular participation in the Kwangju Uprising, I was concerned with explicating its underlying causes:

> Turning to a second approach to the Kwangju uprising, I would like to consider the interpretation of the event's violence, the process of giving meaning to the violence that occurred, on the part of the victims— in this case, the Kwangju citizenry. What sense did people make of it? How did they seek to justify, explain, or excuse what went on, and their own part, collective and individual, in it? What understanding did people have of what they themselves saw or heard or did? Three primary "meanings" or "interpretations" were expressed again and again during the course of the uprising.
>
> The first explanation is that the paratroopers who acted with such apparent random and senseless brutality during the first three days must have been made crazy—hopped up, drugged, drunk, denied sleep and starved into behaving as they did. . . . it was widely reported within the city that the paratroopers had been specially selected and "prepared" for their Sunday afternoon appearance in downtown Kwangju. It was said that their faces were flushed, their breath smelled of alcohol, and they spoke in Kyongsangdo dialect. A published account by a Korean journalist reports:
>
> > "Later I had a chance to talk with a paratrooper who had been captured by the students. I asked him why they had been so brutal. He told me that they hadn't been fed for three days, that immediately before being sent into Kwangju they had been fed *soju* (rice wine) and also that they had been told they were being sent in to put down a communist insurrection"(NACHRK 1980:6).
>
> In the apparent outlandishness of these rumors and allegations about the paratroopers [is] mirrored the incomprehensibility of what people saw taking place around them.[12] The drugged state of the soldiers underscores the innocence of the victims; that they were starved into brutality helps explain how they could have been so violent without any provocation. To the question "What did we do to deserve this?" the answer then is "Nothing." And it is not enough that the paratroopers were reportedly "enemies," from the other side of the country, supporters of the former President and by extension opposed to the political aspirations of Chŏlla-namdo's native son, Kim Dae

Jung. In addition, to do such horrible things they must somehow have been made crazy, been given alcohol, or somehow been put into a state where they could not have been responsible for their own actions. Popular interpretation of the events required the assumption that the perpetrators were not in their "right" minds. For various reasons, the only meaning to be found was in the image of drug-crazed troops run amok.

A second "interpretation" I often heard expressed, one that was articulated in the middle of the uprising and might have been seen as a justification for armed resistance, likens the actions of the government to those of the North Korean communists and/or the Japanese during the colonial period. It was a judge who I first heard say, "What could the North Koreans do to us that would be worse than this?" A May 22 leaflet written by Chosun University students states that "Older people, seeing this brutal genocide, said that it was worse than the communists during the Korean War" (NACHRK 1980:18). And a published eyewitness account, seeking comparison in the past, says "Today's politicians must awaken from the mistaken belief left over from the colonial period that you can overcome any opposition in governing simply by using force and killing" (NACHRK 1980:15).

I would suggest that this drawing of comparisons with the actions of Japanese and North Korean occupiers represented a basic questioning of the legitimacy of the government's actions. To find analogies, people had to look to the worst they had (collectively) experienced—Japanese colonialism, the Korean War—and to the worst they could imagine—North Korean rule. What kind of government would respond with such force, against civilians? Both of the examples represent, to South Koreans, governments that obtained and maintained power through violence and repression—and the illegitimate use of force. Participation in the Kwangju uprising, then, particularly in the mass anti-government rallies of May 24–25, was rationalized as a legitimate protest against the illegitimate use of force. It was the government officials, not the citizens of Kwangju, who were the outlaws.

Finally, a last meaning derives from the oft-repeated expectation that the American government would (and should) actively intervene, to stop the armed confrontation. I myself was angered—and puzzled—by the frequently expressed sentiment that the United States had a responsibility to come to the defense of the city. My notes throughout the period and even for months afterwards make reference to conversations with both friends and strangers about their initial expectations of American support and, later, their surprise and distress at its absence.[13] . . .

Why would people in Kwangju have expected American intervention? To find the answer, we might look at established patterns for the resolution of conflict in Korean society. One key to explaining violent situations, after all, is an understanding of the more usual, more "normal" non-violent outcomes. What is the Korean conflict scenario, the general procedure by which Koreans approach and deal with contentious situations, and the manner in which disputes are interpreted, carried forward, and resolved?

The nature of conflict in Korean society is relatively unexplored territory, at least by anthropologists, except perhaps for the work of Vincent Brandt, who notes that in a village "the sound and fury of conflict is there for all to see" (1971:185) and who draws our attention to its public nature. As a social process, the Korean cultural scenario for conflict resolution involves the public expression of grievances by both sides, as a means of informing the neighbors, of shaping a local consensus, and of mustering popular support for each side in the argument.

It is above all else also a process that relies heavily on the involvement of a third, mediating party for a successful outcome. In fact, it is through the public airing of the dispute that the antagonists solicit the intervention of others. Thus, two men stand in the street yelling at each other as a crowd gathers. When the shoving starts, onlookers step forward to restrain the two, reasoning with them and stopping the fight at the crucial point where verbal aggression threatens to erupt into physical violence. In the same manner, an aggrieved landlady and her equally enraged tenant take turns standing in the courtyard denouncing each other to the world at large in alternating monologues that detail charge and counter-charge. The neighbors listen, and the next day they intervene to prevent the tenant's eviction. Intense verbal aggression and the public expression of grievances serve not as a prelude for physical violence, but function to mobilize third party intervention, to prevent just such an escalation of the dispute.

Perhaps it is not possible to project a model for dealing with interpersonal disputes onto collective political action. But, in the context of such a conflict scenario, the expectation of American intervention in the Kwangju uprising gains new meaning. Like the daughter-in-law standing on the porch pouring out her grievances into the night, people in Kwangju publicly expressed their side of the story, their sense of having been wronged by the government, expressing it first in the form of defensive armed resistance, then in mass rallies and public demonstrations held in the center of town. And, these citizens were surprised when this failed to elicit intervention on their behalf. Public expression of a dispute is interpreted as a call for intervention; the absence of intervention confounds cultural expectations and leaves the means of the conflict's resolution unclear.

Some final observations can be made about these three "meanings." As historical distance from the Kwangju uprising lengthens and the actual event recedes in time, it is assumed that the interpretations of it on the part of the victims are subject to reevaluation, if only on the basis of the new insights and factual information hindsight may bring. But the Kwangju uprising continues to be invested with these interpretations, now reiterated as the innocence of the victims, the illegitimacy of the government's actions, and the culpability of the United States, through its failure to intervene. And, in fact, from the perspective of those opposed to the present Korean government, these "interpretations" have become the most significant aspects of the Kwangju uprising itself (Lewis 1988a:21–25).

Over twenty years (rather than just seven) have now passed since the Kwangju Uprising, and these interpretations remain. The innocence of the victims is now well documented in published eyewitness accounts, visual records, and forensic evidence; details of such atrocities as the Chunam Village Massacre of Innocents, in which students riding in a minibus were ambushed and killed, and the Massacre of Innocents at Chinwŏl-dong, where soldiers shot at children playing by a reservoir (both discussed in Part I), are widely known, and these incidents are featured in victim-centered recountings and materials about 5.18.

More important, in the mid-1990s two popular media portrayals of the events of 1980 served to raise public awareness of the excessive repression and brutality of the Fifth Republic and focus attention on the savagery of the military's actions in Kwangju. A twenty-six episode television drama, *Morae Sigye* (The hourglass), which aired in the spring of 1995 to a vast and attentive public audience, depicted political and corporate power and corruption in the 1980s, including the Kwangju Uprising. The feature film *Kkot Ip* (A petal),[14] which opened in April 1996 during the trials of disgraced former presidents Chun and Roh, was a more poetic (and highly sympathetic) account of May 1980. The film includes a reenactment (by nearly twenty thousand extras) of the demonstrations on Kŭmnamno, although the story focuses primarily on the sexual exploitation of a young girl driven insane by the violence she witnesses.[15] Of particular note was the film's daring use of the national anthem, which is played over images of citizens being slaughtered (Koh 1996:W2). Certainly both of these sensational media representations had an impact on popular consciousness outside of the Honam region about the events of May 1980 and served to subtly alter public perceptions of the Kwangju Uprising.

The 1996 trials—and subsequent convictions—of two former presidents for mutiny, treason, and corruption would seem to firmly establish the second "meaning" of 5.18—that is, the illegality of the government's actions in Kwangju. Surprisingly, though, even after the conclusion of the judicial proceedings, important questions about responsibility for the violence that May remain unresolved. In a 1988 survey in Kwangju, fully 90 percent of the respondents stated they believed the use of excessive force in Kwangju was ordered by "high-ranking government authorities" (*kowi tanggukja*); only 0.5 percent felt it was the result of the actions of individual soldiers (PJC 1988:29). These sentiments were echoed by the prosecution in 1996, when it named Chun as the person responsible for the bloodshed because he ordered the demonstrations quelled (see *Korea Times*, January 25, 1996, p. 2).[16] The court, in turn, effectively upheld this position when it convicted him of treason. However, Chun (and several others) were cleared of separate murder charges in connection with the Kwangju massacre (see *Korea Herald,* August 27, 1996, p. 1).

Thus despite hearings conducted by the National Assembly in 1988–1989, extensive investigation by the prosecution in 1995–1996, and the trial itself, it has never been made clear who gave the order to open fire on civilian protestors, nor has anyone been held specifically responsible for that decision. Chun has consistently denied any involvement with the actions of the martial law forces, claiming he was "outside the loop" and not even responsible for the decision to send troops to Kwangju and that in firing on demonstrators, the soldiers were exercising their legal right of self-defense (see *Korea Times*, May 7, 1996, p. 3). His unremittingly unrepentant attitude has been matched through the years by that of his codefendant, Roh, who created a furor when he remarked before his indictment that "The crackdown of the Kwangju Uprising amounts to nothing compared with the oppression during the Cultural Revolution in China. Hundreds of thousands of people were killed during the Cultural Revolution. But few of those who engineered it were punished" (cited in *Korea Herald*, October 12, 1995, p. 1).

Many people believe questions remain as well about the involvement of the United States in the events of May 1980. The United States maintained operational control of the South Korean army yet failed to act when Chun violated the agreements of joint command in December 1979 and May 1980.[17] Did U.S. officials even try, as they have so vigorously claimed through the years, to restrain Chun as best they could?[18] And why was Chun subsequently invited to the Reagan White House and provided with such visible U.S. support (Cumings 1999:28)? Critics charge—on the basis of now declassified documents obtained in 1995 by Tim Shorrock under the Freedom of Information Act—that "the United States as a matter of the highest policy determined to support Chun Doo Hwan and his clique in the interests of 'security and stability' on the peninsula, and to do nothing serious to challenge them on behalf of human rights and democracy in Korea" (Cumings 1999:24). Or, as Shorrock more trenchantly puts it, "In contrast to the portrait of the befuddled and detached U.S. diplomats portrayed in the White Paper [1989], the [declassified] State Department and Pentagon documents showed that U.S. officials, from the Embassy to U.S. military headquarters, were deeply involved with Chun and the Korean military in planning the crackdown against the popular forces demonstrating in the streets, universities, and factories of the spring of 1980. And they blow away any pretense that U.S. officials were unaware of the key role being played in that crackdown by Chun's special forces" (1999:153).

Thus over twenty years later, the culpability of the United States remains an important part of the meaning of the Kwangju Uprising, although the representation of 5.18 as primarily an act of American foreign policy failure and betrayal is an interpretation that by now is pursued more vigorously outside Korea than by the victims themselves. In 1988 I wrote, "I believe Kwangju will continue to function as an international symbol of the struggle against repressive regimes—especially those supported by the U.S. government—regardless of how the wounds of Kwangju may heal in South Korea. Its power as a symbol can remain, even as the city's image may be altered both on the national political scene, and in the collective identity of the citizens of the Cholla region themselves" (Lewis 1988b:9).

Of course, during the Fifth Republic it would have been difficult to envision the appropriation of 5.18 by the South Korean state, so contested was its meaning—and so potent was its political symbolism. In April 1985, when Chun Doo Hwan arrived in Washington, D.C., on his second official visit to the United States, demonstrations were planned by activist groups to protest U.S. support for the military government in Seoul and to draw attention to opposition to Chun's government.[19] The organizers of the protest had commissioned a poster that simply had "Kwangju" written in *hangul* on top of a red splotch; it appeared on placards held by demonstrators, T-shirts, bumper stickers, and ten billboards around the city.

I had occasion to reference this poster in a paper, "City of Light/City of Outlaws" (Lewis 1988b). The paper offered an analysis of alternative significations of the Kwangju Uprising in the context of the manipulation of regional sentiments and identities in Korea. In the late 1980s it was possible, as well, to allude to 5.18 within the discursive frame of the "problem" of regionalism and to locate the "cause" of the violence in Kwangju in regional prejudices and stereotypes:

> What is so powerful about this image [on the poster]—so evocative that it alone was chosen, in 1985, to symbolize both anti-government sentiments and popular aspirations for democratic reform in Korea? And so powerful too that international human rights activists, Korean-American groups, as well as Koreans in exile in the U.S., could all stand behind it?
>
> If you don't read Korean you may think—as I was told did some Washingtonians who called up local news media to inquire about the message—that it is perhaps a clever advertisement for a new Chinese restaurant. But in fact, it is not. The red blotch represents blood (not spilled plum sauce), and the letters read "Kwangju," the name of a city of about 800,000 in the southwestern part of Korea, the provin-

cial capital of South Chŏlla Province, and the country's fifth largest urban center.

In May 1980 Kwangju and the surrounding countryside was the scene of a major civil uprising. . . . Elsewhere I have written about the uprising itself; today I would like to focus on its aftermath, specifically on competing post–May 1980 representations of the city of Kwangju, of which this poster is an important one. Labeled an insurrection by the government and a massacre by its citizens, the Kwangju Uprising lives on in the popular memory, and the city itself has come to be a powerful symbol in Korean political life, but a symbol that signifies very different things to different groups. Dubbed the City of Light by international human rights activists after a rough literal translation of its name, Kwangju to them represents the failure of U.S. foreign policy in the Third World. Viewed as a center of resistance by the Korean government—a City of Outlaws—Kwangju evokes the historical treachery of the periphery against the state. And to the people of the Chŏlla provinces themselves, Kwangju has become an important part of their collective regional identity, symbolizing a tradition of rebelliousness and embodying the democratic aspirations of all Koreans. I would like to look at these competing views of the city of Kwangju, at the international, national, and regional levels, particularly in the context of the manipulation of regional consciousness in Korea for national political ends.

Compared with other Korean provincial capital cities, Kwangju is unremarkable—except perhaps for the beauty of its natural setting. To the north and west lie the plains of Tamyang and Naju; to the south and east, extensions of the Noryŏng mountain range enclose the city, the highest peak, Mt. Mudŭng, providing a picturesque backdrop for the red tile roofs of Kwangju's densely settled neighborhoods. The urban landscape reflects Kwangju's role as a regional administrative, as well as educational, cultural, and intellectual center. It is a provincial capital . . . [and] contains the provincial capitol building, district court, branches of major banks, offices of national, provincial, and local newspapers, and several institutions of higher education—including Chŏnnam University, the fourth largest public university in Korea. In the middle of town, a long "walking street," thronged day and night with pedestrian traffic, is lined with the city's smartest shops—an island of fashion in the midst of rural Korea, but slightly shabby and countrified in comparison to the cosmopolitan glitter of Seoul's department stores.[20] In 1980 the Kwangju Tourist Hotel offered adequate accommodation for the few foreigners who came to the city on business. An international class hotel has since been built at the foot of Mt. Mudŭng, but the government has not promoted tourism in the region (and Kwangju rarely appears in travel brochures). . . .

The city itself has a long history, dating from the Three Kingdoms' period (4th to 8th centuries), when it was known as Mujinju and belonged to Paekche. During Unified Silla (668–936), the country was divided into nine administrative regions, and Kwangju was designated one of the supervisory cities. And it was during the Koryo Dynasty, in 940, that the city was first called Kwangju. When the system of local administration was reformed in the 1890s, Kwangju was designated a provincial capital.

In terms of the city's relative size, Korea's urban population began to grow during the Japanese colonial period, particularly after 1920; and indeed the population of Kwangju almost doubled, from 12,000 to 23,000, between 1921 and 1925. In the decade after liberation, urban growth continued (Kwangju's population more than doubled in that period, too) although rapid urbanization in Korea really dates from the early 1960s, with the beginning of the government's Five-Year plans to promote export-oriented industrialization; by the mid-1970s, half of all Koreans had become urbanites. Between 1960 [and] 1966, Seoul—Korea's megacity and now home to one-fifth of the nation's population (42 million)—grew more rapidly than did other metropolitan areas, but its relative rate of growth has since slowed, and that of smaller cities has increased. Also noteworthy has been the establishment and massive growth of new industrial cities (as, Ŭlsan and Pohang), but primarily on the southeastern coast.

In contrast, the towns in the southwest, in the Chŏllas, have not been so fortunate. When rapid urbanization in Korea began in post-1960, the region was at a "locational disadvantage for industrial development." The wide, shallow mud flats of the southwest coast—Korea "tilts" towards the Yellow Sea—restricted development of the Chŏlla regions's coastal areas, and the growth of employment opportunities in inland cities, like Kwangju, was not great. Often referred to as Korea's "rice bowl" because of its fertile plains and agrarian character, the Chŏlla area has traditionally been thought of as remote and rural—and

also rebellious, with a history of anti-government political and economic movements that include the Tonghak rebellion of the 1890s,
anti-Japanese resistance in the first part of this [twentieth] century, and
in 1945-6, revolts during the American occupation. And, in the past
decades, as the Chŏllas have lagged behind the rest of the country economically, evidence of regional disparities in development—specifically,
patterns of central government favoritism towards the southeast, the
home region of Korea's last three presidents—has fueled anti-government
sentiment. Incomes in the Chŏlla region had only reached 75% of the
national average in 1975 (and 77% in 1984).[21] When I first went to the
area in 1970, I went over dirt roads on an old country bus. Had I been
going to Taegu, in the southeast, I could have traveled in a new Japanese-
made bus over paved highway. Certainly the perception that the people
of the Chŏlla provinces have not gotten an equal share of the benefits of
Korea's recent miraculous economic growth has caused anger and resentment, and intensified regional rivalries.

To be from Kwangju, then, is first to have suffered, to be historically the victim of regional discrimination, of oppression by the central
government and, more recently, the victim of violence, of a government massacre of innocent citizens. Yet also, the Kwangju spirit of resistance, of righteous rebellion, is a source of regional pride. Natives of
Kwangju are rebels, fighters, engaged in the struggle not just for the re-
dress of regional grievances (both economic and political) but also
against the authoritarian government in Seoul. Regional consciousness
in the Chŏllas has come to signify the larger movement for democracy
in Korea, in opposition to Seoul-based statism; and the events in May
1980 are cast as a national, and not just a regional, tragedy.

In moving to a broader perspective, that of the Kwangju poster
and what might be termed the international human rights community, Kwangju signifies many of the same things. . . . But, in this context, Kwangju stands in opposition to more than just the Korean state.
Bruce Cumings wrote in 1984 that the "rebellion" in Kwangju was not
just against Chun's seizure of power, but "was also against American
support for dictatorship in Korea." It was not just a "Korean episode,"
but "American hands had blood on them too." "At bottom," says
Cumings, " the Kwangju rebellion is a great tribute to the recalcitrant,
struggling people of the Chŏllas, people who demonstrate their humanity by resisting foreign power, economic injustice, and dictator-

ship. Theirs is a proud history, and a lesson to us all." As Chun is responsible for the bloodshed in Kwangju, the city has come to represent the movement for democracy in Korea; but as the U.S. government is also culpable, Kwangju takes on a broader significance, to symbolize the failure of American foreign policy in the Third World. From this perspective, then, Kwangju represents not just one city in Korea with an unfortunate past, but all places around the world touched by U.S. (or other major power) military might and capitalist economic dependency. And the citizens of Kwangju, in turn, symbolize not just the victims of the government's repressive actions, but all people denied basic freedoms and human rights by authoritarian regimes that are supported by U.S. interests.

And traveling to Kwangju, making the "pilgrimage" to the city and graves of its martyrs, takes on meaning not just as a gesture of defiance toward the government in Seoul, but as a demonstration of solidarity with resisters, with those engaged in the struggle against oppression, worldwide. On May 4, 1984, Pope John Paul II made a highly symbolic visit to Kwangju. In 1985, when a delegation of Americans accompanying Kim Dae Jung on his well-publicized return to Korea had trouble confirming hotel reservations in Seoul, one American organizer threatened to hire a bus and go straight to Kwangju from the airport in Seoul—presumably, this would cause the government acute embarrassment. And, in the 1987 Korean presidential election, foreign reporters covering the campaign journeyed to Kwangju to file stories from the symbolic center of the anti-government movement.

Now, finally, what of Kwangju as viewed from Seoul and the national political arena? Traveling to Kwangju has, in the eyes of the government, too, assumed a symbolic importance—so much so that the detention of opposition leaders under house arrest on May 18 so that they cannot attend memorial services in Chŏlla Do on the anniversary of the Uprising is an annual event. The government has, until recently, suppressed public discussion of the Kwangju Incident, as it is called, but in 1985 the Minister of National Defense issued an official report. Rather than a popular uprising or show of regional resistance, the account portrays innocent citizens caught in a situation of protracted anarchy, a city seized by "mobsters" and rioters under the sway of a destructive mob psychology. Kwangju was not a "liberated" city, but a "city of terror," in the control of armed rebels.

Regional sentiments have been evoked by the government too to discredit accounts of a massacre; the Chŏlla tradition of rebellion, as it is used by the government, allows for the dismissal of the event as localized rioting gone out of control. Regionalism also has served to turn popular feeling in the rest of the country against the Chŏlla area—or certainly to deter people from wanting to learn too much about what went on. And finally, by charging Kim Dae Jung . . . with "pulling the strings" in this attempted insurrection by "Communists" and "hooligans," the government raised popular fears about a major opposition political leader. Thus, in the national political context, Kwangju has come to signify the rebelliousness and innate untrustworthiness of the periphery against the state and the treacherous nature of the region itself and its leaders.

Both the government and Kwangjuites used traditional regional sentiments and stereotypes to "explain" the events of May, 1980: "those shifty, lazy people down there, who always oppose the government," or (alternatively) "the people from the southeast have always hated us, they want to kill us all."

Why has this occurred? We can discern in this process the manipulation and intensification of regional differences for larger political ends. Political scientists of Korea point out that in 1967 for the first time there developed an east–west regional split in Korean national voting patterns, with the southeast region voting for its incumbent native son, Park Chung Hee, while Seoul and the Chŏllas voted against him. For the first time geography was the most important determinant of voting decisions. This was in contrast to the previous pattern of voting, of pro-government rural/opposition urban.[22] It is this . . . pre-1967 pattern (urban/rural differences in political attitudes and behavior), this link between urbanization and political opposition that political scientists tend to expect in modernizing nations. Yet, in Korea in the past two decades, the urban electorate has been more likely to support a national political leader from its own region. Or (put another way) regional consciousness has of late been sufficiently strong to have the potential for transformation into a political force in the national arena. And, in [the 1987] presidential election, the regional split was truly stunning: Kim Dae Jung received about 84% of the regional vote and 86% of the votes in Kwangju, while the winner, [Roh] Tae Woo, received about 65% of the provincial vote and 70% of the urban vote in Taegu, his hometown.

It is this issue of regionalism—its rise (or reappearance) in the past decades and the manipulation of regional consciousness to mobilize political support—that is the subject of much interest and concern in Korea today (Lewis 1988b).

In the repressive atmosphere of the 1980s, regionalism provided an answer, for both the victims of government-sanctioned violence and its perpetrators, to the question "Why Kwangju?" The official response to questions about the bloodshed in May 1980 was that it was in Kwangju (and the surrounding Honam region) that public orderliness was threatened. In other words, the military had simply responded with the level of force necessary to maintain stability and control in the face of violent resistance, and the ensuing tragedy was in effect instigated by Kwangju's unruly citizens themselves. From the perspective of the 5.18 victims, of course, the government's excessive brutality in suppressing the demonstrations in their city was part of a larger pattern of regional discrimination against the Chŏlla provinces. As national scapegoats, people in the Honam area could be targeted for just such a crackdown, with little risk of inciting a sympathetic response in other parts of the country.

In the 1990s, in the wake of the success of the popular democracy movement of 1987, the questions about 5.18 and its discursive frame began to shift from "Why Kwangju?" to "Why did the Kwangju Uprising fail?" Conventional wisdom about the achievement of democratic reforms by the end of the 1980s was that for the first time significant numbers of middle-class Koreans were willing to join in the struggle (see Choi Jang Jip 1993:37–39). In hindsight, then, the Kwangju massacre failed to ignite a nationwide democratic uprising in large part because the middle class was too small and too ambivalent to participate (see Sonn 1995:156–179). In short, the Kwangju Uprising was premature.

Events of the summer of 1987 ushered in a new era in South Korea and with it a new image for the city of Kwangju. Political liberalization opened the door for discussions at both the national level and within Kwangju about the meaning of 5.18 and allowed for competing interpretations of the Kwangju Uprising to come into public view (as we shall see).

PART III

Commemorating Kwangju

From Lamentation to Celebration

May—when that day comes again,
In our hearts, blood flows forth.[1]

Kwangju in the 1990s

Oh Kwangju of May! Oh revolutionary Kwangju!
Oh city of youth who band firmly together to fight
Your name eternally, eternally will shine.[2]

ON MAY 17, 1998, I STOOD on Kŭmnamno in front of the Catholic Center in Kwangju, waiting for the Eighteenth Anniversary Pre-Eve Fest event to begin. As usual on this day, the street was closed to traffic, and at the end of the block, against the fountain in front of the Provincial Office Building, a huge stage (almost as wide as the fountain itself) with a gigantic television screen suspended above it (so those in the back could see) had been set up for the annual Eve Fest (chŏnyaje) gala. The stage, the plaza behind it, and the first block of Kŭmnamno, as well as the 5.18 cemeter(ies) in Mangwŏl-dong, would be the sites of many of the main anniversary events to be held in the next few days; this year forty–six different official events were planned during the month-long (May 1–31) commemoration period.[3] In about two hours, at 7:30 P.M., the stage show (typically including several popular singers, a children's chorus, and some sort of 5.18 tribute) was scheduled to begin, and the entire block would be filled with people, either sitting down in the street on scraps of folded newspaper, milling about at the back, or standing crowded along the sidewalks.[4] At that moment, however, the street was rather empty, with only a few hundred spectators gathered around to watch the "event before the main event," which this year was relatively simple and low key: a May *madangguk*, or open-air folk drama, entitled "The

People Who Rose Up" ("Ilŏsŏnŭn saramdŭl"), performed by the twenty-seven-member local troupe Shin Myŏng.

The theater genre *madangguk* first appeared in the late 1960s as part of what became the *minjung* culture movement of the 1970s and 1980s.[5] Based on the aesthetic principles of Korean traditional mask-dance drama, with its emphasis on hierarchical inversion and the use of satirical dialogue, improvisational bantering among the players, and the encouragement of audience participation, *madangguk* is used to generate a sense of communal solidarity and to foster the development of popular consciousness.[6] Along with other reconstructed forms of traditionally marginalized folk culture, such as farmers' music and dance and shamanic ritual performances (*kŭt*)—Korea's "invented tradition of the 1980s" (Kim Kwang-ok 1994:195)—*madangguk* flourished during the Chun Doo Hwan era (particularly on university campuses) as a vehicle for oppositional social and political protest, and peasant rebellion became a popular subject for the performing arts (Kim Kwang-ok 1994:208).[7] As Choi Chungmoo says, "The methodology of the minjung culture movement is essentially a rereading of history as history of the oppressed minjung's struggle and a representation of that history as a paradigm of change. In the history thus reread, hitherto marginalized people enter the central arena of history or become agents of history" (1995:117). *Minjung* imagery celebrates resistance and revolution by the oppressed; naturally, the historical moment about to be reread for us in the performance that day was the Kwangju Uprising itself.

As is customary at such events, a large mat had been put down on the street to demarcate the area representing the "*madang,*" which would function as a stage.[8] A group of musicians with traditional percussion instruments, dressed in the peasant garb characteristic of a contemporary "farmers' band," sat on one end of the mat, and around the other three sides sat the audience, several rows deep. Surrounding this inner circle other spectators stood, jostling each other and trying to shove toward the front for a better view.

I held my ground among the first row of standees and watched the opening scene. It was a familiar folk play scene, enacted in broad pantomime and dance: the wooing of a simpering, hunchback maiden by the slightly drunk village simpleton. The stock antics of the conventional country bumpkin pair drew appropriate chuckles of amusement from the audience, who seemed perfectly content to watch the gently humorous, clichéd little drama play itself out. I, on the other hand, was growing impatient with what appeared to be simply a generic, popularized folk entertainment—what did this have to do with 5.18, I wondered? As I debated leaving, however, the tone abruptly shifted. Nine members of the troupe appeared dressed in bloodstained military fatigues and carrying rifles. Clearly, the Kwangju Uprising narrative was about to unfold.

This scene recounted in dance drama the rebellion's first days: the initial brutality of the government troops, the shock and righteous anger of the citizens, and the subsequent armed resistance by the *simin'gun.* It was followed by a comic interlude that portrayed the period of "Free Kwangju." The heroic *simin'gun* are resting after driving the soldiers out of the city. Two women, marked as lower class by dress (they wear *mompae,* or baggy pants) and speech (they use exaggerated *chŏlla do sat'uri,* or regional dialect),[9] feed them *kimpap* and engage in a humorous boasting contest about which woman's neighborhood has done the most for the struggle; the rebels also then begin a bragging match, retelling their exploits in battle. Familiar characters are represented: the brave young *simin'gun* leader, the high school student who resolves to fight, the young woman who has joined them, and the good-hearted neighborhood housewives who support their cause. The audience is encouraged to participate; with some prodding, we clap our hands and chant along with the *simin'gun*—"Let's get rid of Chun Doo Hwan!" "Let's get rid of martial law!"

Soon the stage is cleared again, and the essentialized peasant couple from the opening scene briefly reappears; now their role in the drama becomes clear: recast as anxious parents, they search in vain for their missing son. The *simin'gun* then return for the well-known final battle scene. We hear the sound of helicopters and the announcement telling citizens to give up their weapons. To applause from the spectators, the *simin'gun* resolve to continue the struggle. When the news comes that the army plans to reenter the city that night, the heroic rebels debate what to do. The high school student refuses to go home and watches in horror as, one by one, his comrades are shot; then he too is killed.

To the sound of *pansori,* the parents return to find the body of their son, who it happens is the *simin'gun* leader.[10] As they mourn, his corpse is draped in a Korean flag and solemnly carried off. In the last scene, nine figures in white hemp *hanbok* smeared with blood—the souls of the martyred dead—appear to perform a final dance sequence rich with traditional imagery of funerals and mourning.[11]

I understood the revolutionary aesthetic of folk theater and the use of this historical event, the appropriation of the 5.18 narrative, as a *minjung* conjuring act celebrating struggle; but it was an event, thus reconstructed, that was also necessarily washed free of its messy complexities, both past and present. As we stood around the imagined *madang* chanting, "Let's get rid of Chun Doo Hwan!," in a chorus directed by the fatigue-clad rebel leader and the bawdy, dancing *ajumŏni*, I could remember that historical moment not just in parody, but also in personal recollection. If I only turn my head, I thought, I can actually see the place where tens of thousands of people really stood together and shouted, "Let's get rid of Chun Doo Hwan!," and I can recall this feeling of righteous defiance and communal resolve. But what about fear? Uncertainty? Danger and a sense of impending disaster? To commemorate is also to forget; those are matters apparently now of only private, not public, memory. I looked around the circle of spectators, searching for middle-aged faces, for others who, while participating in this process of the construction of a particular collective memory of 5.18, might also be old enough to set it beside both their own still vivid personal memories and the realities of their present lives.

In the May *madangguk* performed that day on Kŭmnamno, there was applause when the *simin'gun* decide to fight to the end; yet, as discussed above, the majority of those in the Provincial Office Building that last day chose to leave. The Eighteenth Anniversary Committee chairman himself was a prominent lawyer whose role in 1980 had been as a member of the oppositional (*chaeya*) faction of the Incident Settlement Committee, working to negotiate an end to the uprising by persuading citizens to turn in their guns (KMHRI 1990:179–183); the previous year's chairman was a university professor who had played a similar role (KMHRI 1990:198–202). And while tens of thousands of citizens had battled with government troops in the streets of Kwangju May 19–21, no "righteous army" arose in the early morning of May 27 in response to the *simin'gun*'s call to come out and defend the city.

Of course unlike in the play, not all of those who took up arms were martyred that May; some are now, I thought, perhaps even neighbors of these spectators—not heroic figures but struggling factory workers, petty tradesmen, or (more likely) unemployed middle-aged men.[12] There are women too, like the former street broadcaster—once a *hagwŏn* ("cram school") teacher, now a peddler—who said in 1989 of her life since the Uprising that "In nine years of oppressive existence, I have had many devastating experiences" (KMHRI 1990:911). It is not so hard in Kwangju, especially in May, to find other accounts in lives shattered by 5.18. As the *minjung* retelling of the Uprising narrative was playing on Kŭmnamno, I thought of how its epilogue was simultaneously being enacted in other parts of town, in Kwangju's many sites of memory. At a symposium held the day before by the Injured People's Association, a paraplegic victim in a wheelchair testified about his chronic pain and need for expensive treatment in the United States; that morning, white *hanbok*-clad mothers of the dead publicly grieved at the 5.18 Cemetery at the Bereaved Families' Association annual memorial service; and later in the week members of the Association of the Detained manned an exhibit at the future locale of the 5.18 Freedom Park, where the buildings in which many of them had been held and tried in 1980 would be preserved as an historical site.

The *minjung* reading of May 1980, however, was not the only story told in Kwangju that day. If the oppositional community has since the event embraced the Kwangju Uprising for its *minjung* subjectivity,[13] the state in the late 1990s has commemorated 5.18 for its pro-democracy legacy. What is important in this memorialization of May is not the position of Kwangju citizens as actors who struggled against oppression, but rather the goal—democracy—that they espoused. With the achievement of democratization (marked by the restoration of popular presidential elections in 1987, reinforced by a return to civilian rule in 1993, and finally confirmed by the peaceful change of government in 1998), the Kwangju People's Uprising can be written into the newly constructed national democratization narrative. Reinscribed by the state as the "5.18 Democratization Movement" and retrospectively positioned as a milestone on a journey publicly validated by the state only at its completion, 5.18 had by the end of the 1990s been successfully appropriated by the government; its legacy could be evoked not just in the counterhegemonic discourse of the waning *minjung* movement, but now by the state as well, in the "interest of the nation."[14]

Thus on May 18, the day after I watched the May *madangguk* being performed on Kŭmnamno, I went to see Acting Prime Minister Kim Jong-pil (there on behalf of President Kim Dae Jung) pay his

5.18 Cemetery during anniversary events in 1998. The circular structure to the left is the Photographic Memorial Hall, where portraits of the victims are displayed.

respects at a nationally televised memorial service marking the occasion of the eighteenth anniversary.[15] It was held at the new, monumental 5.18 Cemetery. Since the seats on the vast, open plaza were reserved for hundreds of government officials and bereaved family members, I joined the throngs of ordinary citizens climbing up the grassy slopes enclosing the cemetery in search of a good vantage point. Perched with about a dozen Kwangjuites beside the sunken, flying saucer–shaped concrete roof of the Photographic Memorial Hall, I waited for the event to begin. A military band played numerous refrains of *Pomp and Circumstance* and *The Funeral March* before the acting prime minister, flanked by an entourage of about two hundred dark-suited dignitaries, swept in for the brief ceremony. The national anthem was played, there was a moment of silent prayer, and flowers were laid on the black marble altar that faces the graves; then the prime minister gave the memorial address. In it, he talked about the importance of 5.18 in the nation's history. Reminding the listeners of the country's current financial crisis and the IMF bailout, he asked them to remember the sacrifice of Kwangju's citizens: "What the May 18 democratic fighters might want us to do," he said, "is to discard selfishness and shed sweat of pain for the fatherland."[16]

Kim Jong-pil's statement echoed government appeals to labor unions and a newly emerging association of unemployed people to refrain from violent demonstrations and illegal strikes in the face of a painful corporate and banking restructuring program in which 20–30 percent of workers might lose their jobs (*Korea Times,* May 14, 1998, p. 2). Such protests, the government suggested, would be counterproductive, frightening off foreign investors and thereby exacerbating the jobless problem. For laborers hurt by the nation's economic crisis, then, expressing their frustration through violent street protests would be "selfish"; "self-sacrifice" (as exemplified by the "democratic fighters" of Kwangju) was equated not with struggle against government oppression, but rather with quietly enduring for the good of the nation the personal pain working-class people in particular were certain to face in the period ahead.

It would have been much more difficult, I thought, for the government to thus appropriate the Kwangju legacy and to speak for its victims in the setting of the old cemetery. There the 5.18 narrative could be read in the iconography of the individual graves. Adorned with pictures, keepsakes, and ritual offerings—the accumulated memorabilia of years of public and private mourning—they eloquently told each victim's story. A walk up the small hill through the grave mounds was a journey through May, the dates and faces of the dead calling to mind the stages of the Uprising and the surrounding setting—leftover banners, a pile of stones, the board with pictures of the missing recounting the history of memorialization.

In the nearby new cemetery, to which the bodies were moved in 1997, the individual identity of the "democratic fighters" has been erased, the singular graveside iconography left behind. The pictures are there but enshrined, row upon row, in the Photographic Memorial Hall, where they appear disengaged from the 5.18 text. The Uprising narrative is now told on ten large panels that portray in bas-relief scenes from May 1980 and on two massive larger-than-life statues on the plaza. The *simin'gun,* depicted on one statue as conventionally heroic figures posed on a jeep with guns lifted skyward, bear little resemblance to the exuberant young urban rebels immortalized on a June 2, 1980, *Newsweek* cover: skinny kids with raised fists, hair too long and clad in sweat suits and fatigues, riding through town on a commandeered truck.[17] Upwardly mobile in death, the homogenized images

Cover of Newsweek, *international edition, June 2, 1980.*

on the statue are stripped of the social class markers of the early 1980s. Thus depicted, it was (almost) possible to imagine them, as the prime minister did, as middle-class company employees being asked to tighten their belts without a fuss, rather than unemployed youths and factory workers in the vanguard of a bloody insurrection.

In Kwangju, public memories and private histories of May co-

Statue of Kwangju "rebels" on main plaza of 5.18 Cemetery.

exist; in the rush toward the closure that commemoration brings, it is a place where the bodies of individual citizens still offer a site for resistance to the imposition of a singular 5.18 narrative. It is also constituted as a locale where contestatory representations of the nation's recent history can be enunciated, where *minjung* evocations of struggle against oppression stand uneasily beside the new national chronicle of the triumph of democracy.

Part III is a description of the narratives and practices of commemoration in Kwangju in the 1990s in the context of the various groups and associations that organize and participate in the memorialization process. It is in May in Kwangju when the uneasy coalition of 5.18-related groups, as well as government officials and other citizens' organizations concerned about the image and future of their city, unite under the anniversary banner. The annual celebrations are a prism through which diverse local and national agendas have been refracted and a site where, over the years, the changing signification of the May 18 Kwangju Uprising can be read.

The Construction Of Memory
And the 5.18 Movement

An Overview

THE CHANGING CHARACTER OF MAY in Kwangju, from lamentation to celebration, reflects several things. First and most obviously, it is a consequence of an altered national political context, in which Kwangju has been transformed over twenty years from a site of local memory and mourning to a national sacred place and civic leaders can begin to reimage the city as an Asian "Mecca of Democracy" rather than as the symbolic center of national oppositional political protest and resistance. Certainly the celebratory tone of recent anniversaries follows the achievement in South Korea of a more democratic national civilian government, a shift in official response from cover-up to cooptation, and the concomitant transfiguration of 5.18 from mob riot to heroic struggle.

The dark days of Chun Doo Hwan's Fifth Republic, when even remembering the Kwangju Uprising was a political act, are past; so too is the almost equally unpopular era of Roh Tae Woo.[1] It is even some time now since the establishment of civilian rule in Korea, a transition marked by the appropriation of 5.18 by the government itself: soon after taking office, President Kim Young Sam laid claim on behalf of his administration to the legacy of Kwangju when he noted in a May 13, 1993, statement that as a democratic government, the incumbent regime was an extension of the Kwangju Democratization Movement (cited in *Chosŏn ilbo*, May 14, 1993). Unfortunately, the coda to that declaration—that people in Kwangju should forgive those responsible for the sake of national reconciliation and leave the assignment of blame "to the judgment of history"—was not well received, and in the early 1990s antigovernment sentiment remained strong in Kwangju and the surrounding Honam region. With the announcement on December 22, 1995, of the special prosecution law (to "right the wrongs of the past") and the ensuing trials of former presidents Chun and Roh, however, most civic claims in Kwangju had been answered, and oppositional political fervor weakened. Finally, of course, by the eighteenth anniversary celebration, Kim Dae Jung had won the 1997 election, and Kwangju's native son (and a 5.18 victim) was president of Korea.

From a local, rather than a national, perspective, the "civic festival" atmosphere of the commemoration programs in the late 1990s also represented the emergence in Kwangju of competing claims to the direction and leadership of the 5.18 movement. Ironically, as government censorship of information about Kwangju was relaxed and (beginning in the late 1980s) it became possible within Korea to more freely investigate, analyze, and discuss 5.18, so too could differing points of view on the event's meaning and essential nature be expressed in Kwangju. Kwangju intellectuals, professionals, and civic leaders—citizens who perhaps through guilt as well as caution had remained passive throughout the 1980s—began to vie for a role in the 5.18 movement and a voice in its commemoration.

In many ways this development simply reflects the nascent *minjung/simin* ("people's/citizens") movement distinction appearing in the national political discourse (see Kim Sunhyuk 1996). As Abelmann points out in examining farmer activism in the post-*minjung* 1990s, there was in Korea by the mid-1990s a "widespread fatigue and even disgust" with the culture of dissent. "Many people distance themselves not only from the military authoritarianism of the recent past, but also from the righteousness and drama of dissent—from the totalizing projects of both the left and the right" (1997:250). In Kwangju, the noisy "drama of dissent" has been long playing. And while there is civic pride in Kwangju's identity as a "righteous town" (even city government publications by the late 1990s began to boast of "an historical tradition of spirited resistance against injustice" [Kwangju City 1997:2]), there is also growing public weariness with the city's reputation as a site for the violence of antigovernment demonstrations and their suppression.

As with other social movements in post-*minjung* Korea, the problem for the constituent elements of the 5.18 movement by the late 1990s was how to maintain their own momentum and relative position(s) of power and civic influence in a society in which democratization had been largely achieved.[2] As long as the various 5.18-related groups, as well as most of Kwangju's citizens, shared as a common goal the legitimation of the events of May 1980 and the restoration of the city's honor and national image, the unity and purpose of the movement were assured; naturally, the anniversary events were largely conducted in the antigovernment *minjung* movement idiom characteristic of the 1980s.

But by the 1990s, the national and local political terrain had changed. In Kwangju the new era is marked by the ascendancy of citizens' groups whose purpose and tactics differ from those of the 5.18 victims' associations who claimed ownership of the uprising's legacy in the past through their customary assumption of leadership in the 5.18 movement. While these splits in the 5.18 movement mirror the fault lines in the national political discourse, they also represent (as we shall see) fundamental local differences in perspective about the Kwangju Uprising narrative, the place of various individuals and groups in it, and the civic image Kwangju will carry into the twenty-first century.

Making Martyrs and Patriotic Heroes

Direct Victims' Groups and the Legitimation of 5.18

THROUGHOUT THE 1980s, the construction of a counterhegemonic Uprising story and the work of memorializing 5.18 was largely controlled by those who had suffered the most—that is, the victims and their families. The large number of groups in the broad, loosely defined 5.18 movement are organized on the basis of degree and kind of participation in the Kwangju Uprising, and the competing agendas and fragmentation within the movement since have their origins there too.[1] For the first ten years, leadership came from within the coalition of "directly affected" or "direct victims" groups—that is, associations composed of the three major kinds of victims: bereaved family members, the injured, and those detained/arrested/tried for their role in the Uprising.

During the Chun era, these basic groups splintered as categories became more complicated and refined, in part due to the government's differential treatment (in terms of compensation) of different classes of victims.[2] For example, among the families of those who are missing, some petitions for 5.18 official victim status have been granted by the government and some have not, thus creating two different groups with different claims, interests, and goals vis-à-vis the government and within the 5.18 movement itself.[3] There have also been splits due to ideological and tactical differences.[4] Nonetheless, historically it is the direct victims'

111

power through grief / political risk

groups and their members that have had the most legitimacy, the most power, and the strongest claims to the memory of May 18.

Bereaved Family Members

Mangwŏl-dong's Gatekeepers

A small corner in Zone Three of the municipal graveyard in Mangwŏl-dong (a district a few kilometers north of the city), where most of the victims were buried, was, until the opening of the new 5.18 Cemetery in 1997 (which will be discussed below), the most sacred 5.18 site in Kwangju and served as the symbolic center for mourning and memorialization. Just after the Uprising, on May 29, 1980, the military took victims' corpses there in garbage trucks and dumped them (KCS 1995:5). That day, 126 bodies were buried on the hillside, and a joint memorial service was held; on May 31, 1980, the 5.18 Kwangju Righteous Uprising Bereaved Families' Association (5.18 Kwangju Ŭigŏ Yujokhoe) was formed (BFA 1989:357). Although among the three major direct victims' groups it is not the largest, the group now known as 5.18 Kwangju People's Uprising Bereaved Families' Associa-

Mangwŏl-dong cemetery in Kwangju.

Grave site of a May martyr in Mangwŏl-dong cemetery.

tion (BFA) has been the most influential. This is perhaps because of its claims to and long struggle over the victims' gravesites.

In the early 1980s the cemetery was contested ground as the government tried to prevent people from making it a locus of memory and mobilization. On May 18, 1981, BFA members attempting to hold graveside anniversary memorial rites for the dead were barred from Mangwŏl-dong, and the association's leader, Chŏng Su-man, was detained under the National Security Law (NSL) (BFA 1989:357).[5] Stories are told of students going cross-country over the hills to evade police and reach the cemetery[6] and of visitors to the cemetery being escorted away by the authorities when they tried to assemble (KCS 1995:5). In

1983 the government sought to lessen the power of the site with a plan to relocate the tombs, and victims' families were "encouraged," with offers of up to 10 million won (then about $17,000) and expenses to move the graves (*Korea/Update,* June 1983). The BFA opposed this action, but twenty-six bodies were exhumed and reburied elsewhere.[7]

A record of the BFA's activities during the Chun era, appropriately entitled "A Diary of the Suppression of the Bereaved Families' Association in Its Struggle to Continue the Spirit and Find out the Truth of the Kwangju Massacre" (BFA 1989:357) is a litany of arrests, detentions, and confrontations with police, not only in Kwangju in May, when inevitably there were arrests during attempts to memorialize 5.18 and during demonstrations held in connection with the anniversary, but also during protests in other parts of the country, usually Seoul. In 1986, nine BFA members were taken away by police after a six day sit-in and street demonstration near the Sejong Cultural Center (*Chungang ilbo,* October 24, 1986). Also in 1986, ten BFA members staged a sit-in at the National Council of Churches, demanding that "Those victimized in the Kwangju incident should not be labeled as rioters, and the government should entitle the family members to a pension and other various benefits from the state"; also, they called for an end to government suppression of victims' families (*Chungang ilbo,* October 21, 1986). In August 1988 police took in for questioning all two hundred 5.18 activists who sat in at the entrance to the National Assembly shouting, "Bring to light the truth about the Kwangju Massacre" (*Han'guk ilbo,* August 19, 1988); in November of the same year a BFA member was injured in a demonstration in front of the U.S. Embassy, where he was yelling slogans calling for a public apology from the United States for its role in Kwangju (BFA 1989:360).

Public activism aside, BFA members also suffered constant harassment by the authorities. In particular, they were subject to preventive house arrest, detention, and even abduction by the police whenever the president was visiting the region or there was some reason to fear they might cause trouble. For example, in October 1984 six members were forcibly taken to such cities as Yosu and Taegu and held there in an attempt to thwart a planned memorial service for Pak Kwon-kyŏn (BFA 1989:358); Pak, who had been the president of the Chŏnnam University student council at the time of the Kwangju Uprising, had died in prison two years before. Apparently the practice of abduction and detention of bereaved family members was routine (see BFA 1989:357–359); it is even ironically referred to in one of the victim's memorial pieces (published by the BFA), comparing such "trips" to "*hyodo kwan'gwang,*" or "filial piety excursions," in which children send their parents on a vacation. In remembering Hwang Ho-gŏl, a high school student, the memorial book relates that "His parents couldn't believe their child was dead. They were struck dumb in front of the child's gruesome corpse. His words, telling his mother, Ch'oe Sun-cha, that he would earn money to send them on a *hyodo kwan'gwang,* still ring in her ears. And now, as Ho-gŏl was killed, this *hyodo kwan'gwang* has become a disgraceful act of oppression, in that everytime Chun Doo Hwan comes to Kwangju, the bereaved families are taken elsewhere, by force" (BFA 1989:230).

It was not until the fifth anniversary, in 1985, that Kwangju citizens could freely visit Mangwŏl-dong. In the spring of that year, with the inaugural session of the Twelfth National Assembly, the once taboo topic of Kwangju was for the first time a matter of public discourse, and the city of Kwangju and its "sacred places," particularly the cemetery, had become a highly emblematic political battleground, the site not just of a local tragedy, but also the locus of the national democracy struggle itself.[8] This ongoing linkage between 5.18 and other broader based social movements was reinforced when, from the late 1980s, thirty-one bodies of other "democratic martyrs" (victims of state oppression who died or were killed in the democratization/social justice movement of the time) began to be interred in Mangwŏl-dong too, in what was now the "5.18 Democratization Cemetery." These additional tombs increased the symbolic value of the cemetery as a national, and not just regional, sacred place.

Where once the government had kept out Kwangju's mourners, now the BFA acted as "gatekeeper" to the 5.18 burial site. In December 1987 then presidential candidate Roh Tae Woo canceled a plan to pay tribute at Mangwŏl-dong after about twenty BFA members staged sit-ins in opposition to the proposed visit (*Tonga ilbo,* December 3, 1987); in 1989, when Roh as president was scheduled to visit Kwangju on an annual inspection tour, nine 5.18-related organizations held a press conference and issued a statement vowing that "We will employ every possible means to oppose President Roh's visit to Kwangju because of his failure to ascertain the truth of the Kwangju incident and to punish those responsible for the Kwangju Massacre" (*Choson ilbo,* February 15,

1989). The threat of serious demonstrations and physical violence was not an idle one: in 1989 ruling party dignitaries were roughed up by 5.18 group members after going to the cemetery (*Tonga ilbo*, March 11, 1989). In March 1993 (and again in 1994) President Kim Young Sam was prevented from paying homage as well.

It was not only Korean government and ruling party officials who encountered hostility and resistance in Kwangju. In 1990 U.S. ambassador Donald Gregg made a trip to the city for the stated purpose of removing Kwangju citizens' misunderstandings of U.S. involvement in 5.18 and alleviating anti-American sentiments in the region (*Segye ilbo*, January 9, 1990), but many 5.18 movement figures refused to meet with him, including Chŏn Kye-ryang of the BFA, who was quoted as saying, "The United States maintains that it did not intervene in the Kwangju Uprising, but even children would not believe that. Now it is trying to justify its actions, which is tantamount to dishonoring Kwangju citizens and to killing Kwangju once again" (*Tonga ilbo*, January 11, 1990). The atmosphere surrounding Mangwŏl-dong in particular was sufficiently politicized and intimidating into the mid-1990s that even the American director of the ACC, who lived in Kwangju from 1993 to 1995, never visited the grave sites.[9]

If exclusion from the cemetery was a symbolic act, paying tribute at Mangwŏl-dong was equally significant. Pope John Paul II journeyed to Kwangju on May 5, 1984, as did small numbers of foreigners, primarily human rights activists and journalists. On September 8, 1987, Kim Dae Jung went to Mangwŏl-dong and met with BFA members; crowds of up to five hundred thousand greeted him on his first visit to Kwangju in sixteen years (*Chosŏn ilbo*, September 9, 1987).

After 1989, when the Kwangju Uprising could be legally commemorated for the first time, the most prominent event in the anniversary program, the memorial service for the victims (*hŭisaengja ch'umosik*) on May 18, was held at the burial ground.

Public Spaces/Private Rites

By 1995, on the fifteenth anniversary, crowds of up to reportedly ten thousand (*Kwangju ilbo*, May 18, 1995) gathered at 10 A.M. for the annual memorial service. The major television networks had set up desks amid the grave mounds for their news anchors, and camera crews seeking a panoramic view of the huge spectacle perched atop a towering

BFA memorial service on May 17, 1998.

crane. The service opened with the national anthem and included a memorial poem, speeches by 5.18 dignitaries, and music by the Kwangju City traditional music orchestra. The main part of the event, however, was a Confucian-style memorial ceremony, conducted in the form of a traditional ancestral rite (*chesa*).[10] The large altar at the foot of the cemetery in front of the graves was covered with food offerings as for a death-day ritual; the officiants, clad in traditional Korean ceremonial garb over their black suits, burned incense and offered wine to summon the spirits. The mayor of Kwangju, appearing for the first time at this graveside service, was one of the participants, along with a representative of the Anniversary Events Committee and the head of the 5.18 coalition's central committee. At the conclusion of the formal rite, a large group of invited guests seated on the dais—a collection of civic leaders that included local politicians, university administrators, and religious figures—approached the altar one by one to burn incense and leave floral offerings. The official program ended with an invitation for ordinary citizens to come forward to pay their respects, and indeed people continued to mill about in the cemetery for several hours afterward as relatives of the dead gathered around the altar and the graves, preparing more food and then sharing a meal.[11]

Commemorating Kwangju

While a detailed analysis of the structure of this annual ritual is beyond the scope of this chapter, several observations can be made about its form and meaning and its displacement, after the move to the new cemetery in 1997, from the central spot on the anniversary program. Most obvious are the ways in which the ceremony resembles Confucian-style death-day ancestral rituals: spirits of the dead are called; wine, incense, and food are offered; participants bow; and the ritual is conducted on the death anniversary.[12] There are also, however, many other ways, both small (for example, it is held during the day) and large (children who predecease their parents are not memorialized, and at Mangwŏl-dong the officiants are not in the proper line of lineal descent) in which it does not. At the very least, domestic ancestral rites in Korea are private family affairs, while this is a community event. How have these traditional Korean ceremonies for the dead come to be transformed in Kwangju every May 18 into a public communal ritual of mourning?

Certainly (as noted above), in the *minjung* culture movement of the 1980s it was commonplace in Korea to see the use of traditional folk cultural elements in rituals of resistance and political protest, particularly on college campuses. Although this primarily involved the appropriation of shamanic practices, public funerals or rituals evoking funeral imagery often mixed in Confucian rites (see Kwang-ok Kim 1994:197, 214). Thus the choice of a Confucian-style ceremony could be seen simply as a political statement, a self-conscious display of oppositional sentiment in the popular culture movement idiom.[13]

But this was not a ritual performance staged by activist students on a college campus; it involved mourning relatives and civic leaders, so despite its *minjung* movement overtones, perhaps the intent (conscious or otherwise) really is the evocation of Confucian (rather than folk cultural) values. Confucian imagery is often used in Korea to symbolize morality, legitimacy, and virtue. And while traditionally the performance of ancestral rites was about the solidarity of agnatic groups, it also "dramatized . . . the fundamental morality of the participants" (Lee Kwang-kyu 1987:56).[14] A customary Korean measure of virtue is the observance of proper ritual form; thus by honoring the 5.18 dead in this way, Kwangju citizens demonstrate their own rectitude.

The use of Confucian rituals at Mangwŏl-dong then becomes an implicit critique of a government that would suppress the memories of 5.18 and through much of the 1980s would characterize those buried at the cemetery as hoodlums, rioters, and Communists.[15] The rite on May 18 asserts the basic righteousness of the actions of those who died and underscores the importance of remembering them properly in death; at the same time, it is a testament to the virtue of those who participate in the ceremony.[16]

It is interesting to note in this regard that in looking at shamanic rites and memories of the April 3 Uprising (1948) in Cheju, Seong Nae Kim found that relatives were afraid even to memorialize the dead by performing *chesa* because to do so would implicitly pose a political challenge to "the official discourse that has kept the secret of this event to itself" (1989:255).[17] People in Cheju "plainly had to accept forgetting that event as a cure for its trauma" (p. 255), and it is only in shamanic healing rites that repressed memory of the political violence of 1948 was allowed to surface (p. 251). In contrast, in Kwangju throughout the 1980s and early 1990s, the memorial rites on May 18 at Mangwŏl-dong served to publicly perform a different truth claim than the official histories, to symbolically posit a counterhegemonic version of 5.18 to which not only the bereaved relatives but also the larger community could subscribe.

What is usually a private familial event here assumes a public purpose—and perhaps more than just a political one at that. Rituals are also used to evoke certain sentiments; by performing these death-day ancestral rites (including weeping openly beside the graves) every year on May 18, mourners in Kwangju create the feelings they evoke for new groups of observers. Perhaps these services allow others to participate, and by recreating their sorrow and publicly displaying it each May, the bereaved in Kwangju keep their grief fresh and pass it on.

There are in fact a number of communities participating simultaneously in these rites. Beyond those who have some relationship with the dead, there are the many local citizens who have a personal connection to 5.18 and the events of May 1980, as well as officials of the city and regional government. Although until recently representatives of the national government have been explicitly excluded from these memorial rites, people—particularly young people—do come from other parts of Korea to watch the service. Korean university students who in 1996 traveled with me to the anniversary events in Kwangju expressed the idea that as students, they felt an obligation to make the trip—like a pilgrimage to a sacred place. Many told me they felt guilty they had not visited Kwangju before; it was as if there was a gap in their college experience, even though some clearly felt ambivalent about being there.[18] But in the intimacy of the old Mangwŏl-dong cemetery, the May 18 memorial service was an emotionally moving event indeed for those who attended.

Finally, the meaning of this Confucian-style ritual may be found in what it was not—that is, its form may be determined by the possible cultural alternatives. For example, it did not mimic civic memorial services as customarily conducted under government auspices. This could only become apparent, perhaps, in 1997, when the event on May 18 changed significantly. With the opening of the new cemetery that year, the BFA's community *chesa* was displaced from the actual death anniversary to May 17; in its place, the government held its own "5.18 Democratization Movement Memorial Service" (5.18 Minjuhwa Undong Kinyŏmsik) on May 18. Although the relatives of the dead sat in places of honor, it clearly was not their event. Sponsored by the central government rather than the local anniversary events committee, the short, thirty-minute ceremony included a moment of silence, a proclamation of the National Commemoration Day, and the paying of respects not just to the 5.18 dead, but (by extension) to all patriotic martyrs and national heroes. The large number of government officials present stepped forward in groups to place flowers on the altar, while a military band played a dirge.

Any observers accustomed to the informal atmosphere, casual starting time, and greater length of the previous years' services would have missed this event entirely: the program began promptly, and seating on the large, open plaza was limited. By the next year the government's service featured a speech by the prime minister, access to the plaza was restricted to dignitaries, and many of the reportedly ten thousand who came to watch (*Chŏnnam ilbo*, May 18,1998, p. 1) had to view the spectacle from perches on the grassy slopes of the cemetery's margins. In contrast, the bereaved families' traditional rite, again held on May 17, drew only a few hundred people.

In analyzing the rites in Hiroshima commemorating the atomic bombing of that city, James Foard looks at how those rituals, grounded in traditional Japanese practices regarding the dead, have evolved into "an array of symbolic actions" that address a national, and even international, community. In Hiroshima, "what was familial and local became public and universal" (1994:19). This is not to suggest that Japanese funeral and ancestral rites are the same as Korean ones or that the transformative process has been the same in Kwangju as in Hiroshima. What is useful about Foard's analysis is his delineation of participant communities (those personally connected with the dead, the city, the Japanese nation, and the world) on the basis of their relative particularity and universality (pp. 33–34). For Foard, "it is the discourse among groups of differing degrees of particularity and universality that has articulated the issues of legitimacy in the ritual space of Hiroshima" (p. 31). As he notes, "The relationships among these categories of communities revolve around questions of legitimacy and hence authority to define meaning. In general, the more universal concede greater legitimacy to the more particular" (p. 34).

In the case of the 5.18 commemorations and Kwangju's ritual spaces, then, if the central memorial service on May 18 were to retain elements of the traditional Korean ancestral rites, priority would have to be granted to the more particular, smaller group of bereaved relatives and to the local citizens who have personal connections to the event. These annual graveside rituals have been a means through which these communities could symbolically assert their claims to legitimacy and hence their control over the essential meaning of the Kwangju Uprising. However, with the reinterment of the 5.18 dead in the new ritual space of the government-supported 5.18 Cemetery and the establishment of the anniversary date as a national commemoration day, the national government has appropriated the event, and rather than attempt to contend with the local community for control of the customary Confucian-style traditional rites, the state has simply replaced them with a civic memorial service of its own. In this way, the government has at the same time assumed the authority to define meaning as regards the Kwangju Uprising.

The chairman of the Seventeenth Anniversary Events Committee explained the dilemma confronting the local community:

> The *kinyŏmsik* [memorial service] is a national government thing, right? It isn't something our anniversary events committee does, so if on that day we were to put together the government's *kinyŏmsik* and the BFA's *ch'umoje* [commemoration ceremony], it would seem a little

strange, so the BFA's *chesa* day was advanced a day and . . . certainly having it earlier is a good thing. It's just that having it on that day is also desirable, and now it is put ahead. . . . If we look at it in terms of the past, we can't help but feel that that event is more important than the national memorial day event, so in that place [the cemetery] the *ch'umoje* is no less consequential. If for some reason between the two, we drop one, it won't please the other, will it? But if we say, let's have the *kinyŏmsik* in the morning and the *ch'umoje* in the afternoon, surely it will fall a little flat (personal communication, May 21, 1997).

This shift from the central spot on the commemorative events calendar certainly is symbolic of the BFA's displacement from power in the late 1990s. With no further agenda beyond what has already been achieved, it is difficult to imagine how the BFA can maintain its privileged place in civic affairs. Ironically, the very success of the bereaved families, as evidenced in the monumental scale of the new cemetery and its tacit recognition of the 5.18 dead as national heroes, precludes any further demands, and the concomitant cooptation by the government of a major role in the memorialization process forecloses any immediately apparent opportunities for (even symbolic) leadership. While the BFA's 1997 official anniversary message (*kungminege tŭrinŭn kŭl*) concludes with the statement that "There are still many tasks that remain in order for the 5.18 People's Uprising to become the foundation for this country's democracy and an important experience that leads toward world peace and the expansion of human rights," it outlines no concrete goals or plan of action for the coming year.

Empty Graves For Mourning Mothers

There are, however, other categories of 5.18 bereaved relatives who still have an agenda and claims to make on the government. There is, for example, Mrs. Kwang-ok Chŏn, whose nineteen-year-old college student son disappeared in May 1980; when she and her husband could not find him by June, they reported him missing. He was number 211. For three years they searched for him and in 1985 officially registered him as a presumed 5.18 victim. In November of the same year, the government ruled there was no evidence linking their son to the Uprising, so he was not one of the forty-seven people officially recognized as victims whose bodies had not been recovered. Mrs. Chŏn began attending the BFA meetings anyway and soon became an active member. The group met twice a month, and at the second meeting it went to the Mangwŏl-dong cemetery. This made a big impression on Mrs. Chŏn, who felt that her most serious sin as a mother was not being able to bury her son (see below). In 1987 she finally erected an empty grave mound for her child. As she testified in 1988, she knows her son died at the hands of the soldiers in Kwangju, but if she could only know where they buried him, she would be satisfied (KMHRI 1990:1272–1273).

Mrs. Chŏn's story highlights some of the differences separating— and issues remaining for—people in Kwangju who have in common the loss of a loved one in the Uprising. Those like Mrs. Chŏn who have no remains to support their death claims confront both legal and emotional problems. The lack of a body to properly honor in death, or the possibility of a violent end, or to die unmarried or childless or before one's parents—all are situations not to be taken lightly in Korea, where restless ancestors and hungry ghosts ("the unquiet dead") are a common source of affliction for the living (Kendall 1985:99–102). When "in the care and feeding of ancestors . . . life does not follow ideal forms" (p. 149)—that is, when parents do not live to an old age and die peacefully, to be honored in ancestral rites by filial sons—families are exposed to supernatural dangers. As Kendall notes of the perils of "hungry ghosts," "Because they are not entitled to *chesa* food, ghosts are perpetually hungry. . . . Because they died unsatisfied, they wander angry and frustrated, venting their anguish on the living (p. 99)." Mrs. Chŏn has much to fear, indeed, from the restless ghost of her unfortunate son.

The Missing People's Association (Haengbulchahoe—MPA) is composed of the families of assumed victims whose bodies have still not been recovered. Some of them, like Mrs. Chŏn, identify with the BFA; certainly for the relatives of the few dozen (or about one-third) of the reported missing who have been granted victim status, the cemetery (and monetary compensation) provide some comfort. In the old Mangwŏl-dong burial plot a large billboard was set up with pictures of the official missing, and their families could come there to mourn. In the new 5.18 Cemetery, these victims are honored in a special section with headstones and empty grave plots (with no mounds) for each.

For many of the relatives of the missing, finding the bodies of their loved ones remains a major concern; in fact, in Kwangju in the late 1990s the question of *ammaejang*, or secret burials, was one of the important unresolved 5.18 issues. It is widely believed that the military dumped corpses in unmarked graves; the belief is kept alive by the number of missing still unaccounted for after so many years, as well as by the periodic discovery of bodies at construction sites. Rumors abound about where such burial grounds might be. For example, MPA members point out an area behind the military hospital where bodies of the injured who died while in custody were reportedly hidden. The story is told that a backhoe operator was ordered to dig a ditch, then asked to turn around and close his eyes; after some time, he was ordered to fill in the ditch. After the operator's death a few years later, his widow repeated the tale. At another suspected site, along a riverbank behind a former military base, the bodies of two 5.18 missing turned up when pilings were driven for a new bridge.[19]

The difficulty with recovering more bodies is, first, knowing where to dig. While one or two conscience-stricken soldiers have come forward to reveal where they buried their victims, in general Kwangju citizens have been unsuccessful in discovering the truth about *ammaejang*. It has been suggested that offering some reward (*hyŏnsanggŭm*) for each body recovered might provide a sufficient incentive, but there are budgetary problems with this suggestion.[20] Financial concerns are a second barrier to investigating possible secret graves. It takes considerable resources to properly excavate such sites, and the MPA is not a large group. In addition to the 47 official missing, there are another 102 registered but unrecognized missing. And although (as suggested above) some people assume there may be as many as 100 more unregistered missing, these "unnoticed missing" obviously have no relatives to lobby for the recovery of their bodies two decades later. It should also be noted that there are some corpses that have never been positively identified. Again, sophisticated forensic analysis requires money and a willingness on the part of the government to resolve the issue (Lee Jae-eui 1995:100); these victims may also be among the "unnoticed missing."

The Recently Bereaved

While those who mourn their missing children may seek solace with the BFA, another category of grieving relatives, those whose family members have died since May 1980, are more closely aligned with the

hosts of mourners (annotation) associations

5.18 injured. There is a Bereaved Families' Association for Those Who Died after 5.18 composed of relatives of the additional 120 victims who have died since 1980.[21] As the chairman of the group said in support of a proposed treatment center for the injured, "Among the wounded who have died it is clear that the many mysterious or accidental deaths at a young age are from mental illness and suicidal depression resulting from injuries caused by such things as bullet wounds, beatings, and torture. Wouldn't they be able to live a bit longer if their living conditions were good and they received continuous medical treatment? . . . Those who died afterwards suffered many times the pain of those who died at the time—and then they died" (Kim Sŏng-su 1997:16).

Of the deaths between 1980 and 1997, over half (sixty-nine) were gunshot victims in their twenties and thirties, and surprisingly few (only seventeen) were older people in their sixties and seventies (Kim Sŏng-su 1997:17). The association attributes many of these untimely deaths to the despair the injured feel over their inability to work and the financial devastation their bad health and medical needs wreak on their households (Kim Sŏng-su 1997:15; also see Lee Jae-eui 1995). Thus their families identify with the issues of the Injured People's Association, which has helped many of them in the past.

Those who die of 5.18-related causes are eligible to be buried in the 5.18 Cemetery—there is a great deal of empty space for just this purpose—although only thirteen actually rested there in 1997. Most are scattered in family plots throughout the city and the region, although there were plans to exhume and reinter some in the new cemetery after the seventeenth anniversary (Kim Sŏng-su 1997:15).

The Injured

It is good that there is room left in the 5.18 Cemetery since of the 3,416 official victims (*injong toen p'ihaeja*), the majority (over 95 percent) are survivors of one kind or another who continue to suffer from the events of May 1980.[22] Research has shown that over 92 percent of 5.18 victims evince posttraumatic stress disorders (Byun 2000:146). Among the victims, 42 percent suffer from physical ailments, 19 percent from mental problems, and 31 percent from both (Byun 2000:147–148); in addition, their degree of life change events, anxiety, and depression is

7.1, 3.2, and 2.7 times higher (respectively) than nonvictims in Kwangju (Byun 1996).

The victims are also in general less educated and poorer than average. About 70 percent of the casualties were working class (factory workers, service sector laborers, petty traders, farmers) or unemployed, and evidence suggests the same is true for 5.18 survivors (PJC 1988:53). Furthermore, throughout the 1980s, the direct victims tended to remain poor, with many actually suffering downward mobility (PJC 1988:52). In Byun's (1996) 1995 sample of victims, 32.35 percent were jobless in 1980, but the proportion had risen to 64.71 percent in 1995. While these figures do not control for many variables, it is clear that the socioeconomic status of the victims (and their families) has in general deteriorated since the Uprising. Byun's observation that these people have "for the past 17 years and even now . . . been confronting death" (1997: 8) is not empty rhetoric: since 1980 an additional 120 of the wounded have died (as we have seen); survivors are at greater risk for drug addiction (from pain killers), alcoholism, and suicide (Lee Jae-eui 1995:82–107); and family members of the 5.18 dead and missing are more likely to suffer associated deaths, often from *hwabyŏng*.[23]

The 5.18 Injured People's Association (IPA) was the second victims' group founded, on June 13, 1982 (Kwangju City 1997:143). As with the other groups, association leaders claim higher victim numbers than the official government count, reckoning 4,326 were injured in May 1980 (Byun 1997). It is assumed that many victims, particularly of socially embarrassing crimes such as rape, have been afraid to come forward; certainly in the 1980s to be a 5.18 victim was self-stigmatizing. Group membership has steadily dwindled over the years as the wounded have either gotten better or died. One member, now bedridden, reminisced about how at first the injured, mostly young and unemployed, used to help each other, even pushing each other's wheelchairs around. By the mid-1990s, however, there were only "about 300" in the association.[24]

The injured, like the bereaved family members, have a long history of 5.18-related activism, although IPA leaders are sensitive to being upstaged in the public imagination by the BFA. In fact, so thoroughly is the 5.18 movement as a whole identified with the BFA that a leader of the IPA complained at a meeting of the group that when the different 5.18-related associations were jointly sending members to Seoul in 1996 to attend the Roh and Chun trials, the bereaved families got all the credit:

> People believe only the IPA "struggles" [*t'ujaeng hada*]. Now in front of the courthouse, reporters from 11 broadcasting companies and newspapers think all the people coming to Seoul are members of the IPA—but they put us in the newspapers as "the BFA and other 5.18-related groups." So last time they asked me something, I shouted at them, saying "Unless you put the IPA first, don't talk about me in your newspaper." They said, "You want too much!" So now if you look at the major papers—if you really look at the *Tonga ilbo*—they now say "5.18 IPA and other related organizations." Always we go first—we made a big fuss (October 19, 1996).

The speaker went on to say that there were some problems, though, in being the main group. He related an incident where BFA members created a ruckus in the courtroom and the judge ordered them all to leave: "So BFA members make noise, and the IPA is blamed. There are advantages to having our name at the top but also a bad side," he concluded.

Before the campaign to prosecute those responsible for the Kwangju Massacre, the IPA was also involved in the late 1980s in the struggle to bring to light the truth about the Kwangju Uprising; for example, on July 9, 1990, about three hundred group members held a rally in support of a special law about 5.18 including demands that the facts be revealed, those responsible be punished, the reputation of Kwangju citizens be publicly restored, memorial projects be undertaken, and victims be compensated (ICNDK 1990:12).

The call for compensation was of special concern to the IPA. As with the families of the deceased, in the summer of 1980 those who were injured received some compensation (100,000 W each) from private donations and promises of money for medical treatment (Pak Wonsoon 1995:30). In 1988, when 5.18 was again on the national agenda, there was a period of open registration, during which 704 victims came forward to officially register claims with the government (10 dead, 581 injured, 102 missing, and 11 miscellaneous); 550 of them were granted. Finally, in 1990, the first compensation plan (*1 ch'a pusang*) was passed by the government, and 142 billion, 700 million W was given to 2,227 people. In a subsequent second compensation plan *(2 ch'a pusang)* under the Kim Young Sam administration, an additional 2,750 victims decided to register claims, including 16 dead, 118 missing, 764 injured at the time and 714 hurt in custody, and 1,138 detained. Of these, 50–60 percent were denied for lack of evidence, but 37 billion, 900 million W was eventually distributed to 1,831 people (Pak Wonsoon 1995:31–32). These two government compensation efforts have been somewhat controversial, with many claims being denied and some groups of direct victims refusing (as we shall see) on principle to accept the money and/or opposing the giving of monetary awards.

In the late 1990s, with the successful achievement of so many of the 5.18 movement goals, the IPA's primary focus has become medical treatment *(ch'iryo)*: getting adequate care, paying for it, and living with the effects of chronic illness and disability. Although most of the injured have health insurance, in the majority of cases it does not cover all medical expenses (Pak Yŏng-sun 1998); those who are disabled also have difficulty finding work and must be supported by their spouses and families.

Many of the victims also suffer from chronic pain from bullet splinters (or fragments) left in their bodies, for which the only relief is increasingly larger doses of drugs. Kim Yong-dae, whose spinal cord was severed, says the bullet splinters are like scattered sand, impossible to remove (at least without treatment outside Korea) but causing pain as his blood circulates. The pain is still 50 percent as much as when he was first hit, and his biggest wish "is to have my kid go to college. And then, before I die, if my pain could be gone for even one day, I would have nothing else to wish for. Because my body hurts so much, I can't help but think about that time [1980]. Whether I am active or not . . . the broken nerves, spine, my lower body will not recover. I don't expect that. But to the extent that the pain stops—for a day or a week—it seems impossible until I die" (personal communication, 1996). Another common medical problem is lead poisoning (from bullets); this has had an impact on victims' general health, although for many years they were not even aware of it.[25]

Several of the critically ill would benefit from treatment in U.S. trauma centers, and the IPA did manage to send three victims to Los Angeles in 1996. Two of them were children in 1980. One, Park Sang-chul, was shot in the back and after ten operations in Korea still suf-

Kim Yong-dae at third annual IPA symposium, May 16, 1998.

fered from partial paralysis and an open wound in his back that would not heal (Kang 1996:B1). Unfortunately, the group has had great difficulty raising even the relatively small amount needed to send several more of the seriously injured overseas for medical treatment.

Needless to say, caring for the victims is also stressful for their families, who may in turn need financial and psychological support. As Kim Yong-dae says of his own faithful partner, "For my wife, it must be like being in a grave. It is a mystery to me why the center of her heart has not exploded by now."[26] His wife, Lee Hwa-sil, was one of four "angel wives" (*ch'ŏnsa anae*) given the May Women's Award in 1995 for devotedly supporting their bedridden husbands (Lee Jae-eui 1995:89).

To address these problems, in 1996 the IPA began, as its part of the Uprising anniversary events, to hold an annual scholarly meeting (*haksul daehoe*), the purpose of which was to educate the public about issues related to the injured and as a forum for presenting the group's agenda. At the first one, on May 25, 1996, the results of research on the victims' health after fifteen years were discussed. The second, in 1997, was devoted to the presentation of a concrete proposal for a comprehensive treatment/public welfare center for 5.18 victims (*ch'iryo mit chaehwal pokchi sent'ŏ*);[27] the third, in 1998, focused on the feasibility of seeking compensation for psychological damages. By labeling these events "scholarly," presenting factual information and sound arguments in a scientific context, and soliciting the help of locally/regionally recognized (nonvictim) academics, the group hopes to depoliticize its agenda and win broader public support. As one professor said to IPA leaders at an informal dinner after one such May meeting as the panel participants were assessing how the event had gone, "You IPA members need to learn now how to do more than just this," pumping his fist up and down in the air in the familiar Korean protest gesture commonly made at antigovernment demonstrations and rallies. These scholarly meetings represent new tactics, consciously adopted by the IPA in an effort to share in the new-found national legitimacy of the Kwangju Uprising and to compete for the public money that is as a result available since the late 1990s for 5.18-related projects.

Unfortunately, the fact that the IPA scholarly meetings have been attended by a relatively small number of people (fewer than two hundred) who are mostly victims themselves and that the organizers have had difficulty finding academics and medical professionals willing to help is indicative of the general antipathy in Kwangju toward the injured. Despite the compelling argument that if the 5.18 spirit means respect for human dignity, taking care of the victims should be a civic priority, most citizens prefer to have 5.18 be "over."[28] Certainly the public perception is that the injured had by the late 1990s been adequately compensated for their pain. Thus the IPA struggles to articulate the injured's unmet needs in a less than receptive civic environment. Ironically, the trials of former presidents Chun and Roh in 1995 (which, as we have seen, the victims' groups actively sought and attended) helped provide just such a public sense of closure and make it harder for the group to solicit support.

Those Detained/Arrested/Tried

Without love, or honor, or even a name to pass on,
One's whole life to push forward, a fervent pledge.
Our comrades are gone, and only a banner waves;
Until a new day dawns, let's never waver.
Awakening, we call out, a fervent battle cry.

I'll go on ahead, and you, the living, follow!
I'll go on ahead, and you, the living, follow!
—From "A March for My Beloved," a popular May song

In 1996 I dodged dump trucks and sank ankle deep in red Chŏlla soil on a mission to see the former Sangmudae courtroom and jail. I was following a "Keeping the 5.18 Spirit Alive" Sacred Sites Pilgrimage (*sŏngji sullye*) outlined in a brochure put out by the Fifteenth Anniversary Committee; a map was provided for a self-guided tour of important 5.18 sites in Kwangju, including the courtroom and jail, on what had been in 1980 a major military base at the western edge of town. It was here that the Martial Law Branch Headquarters for North and South Chŏlla Provinces had been established. By 1996, however, the military base was gone and a huge housing complex, Sangmu New Town, was being developed on the land, so I wandered through a vast construction site of row upon row of as yet uncompleted high-rise apartment buildings before finding the small area, enclosed by a barbed wire fence and overgrown with weeds, of one-story structures where detainees had been held and tried in May 1980.

These buildings were to be preserved for later reinstallation in the May 18 Theme Park and Memorial Park being developed in Sangmu New Town. Part of a larger Kwangju Memorial Project (which includes the new 5.18 Cemetery and a Memorial Hall and Square projected for downtown), the parks are intended to "provide people with a place to reflect [upon] the historic meaning of the struggle and to incorporate the May 18 spirit in their daily life" (Kwangju City 1997:16). It is the section of the park where the Sangmudae courthouse and jail will be housed (dubbed "5.18 Freedom Park"—5.18 Chayu Kongwŏn) that is the particular memorial domain of the Association of the Detained (5.18 Minjung Hangjaeng Kusokcha Hoe)—or AD.[29] By May 1998 Sangmu New Town was inhabited (and the roads paved), although the 5.18 Memorial Parks had yet to be completed. Nonetheless, the AD, as its part in that year's anniversary events, set up an exhibit of drawings of the future memorial space and a Kwangju Uprising picture display in a tent near to where the 5.18 Freedom Park would be located.

If those injured in May 1980 point to the bereaved families and say they have gotten too much, those who were detained/and or tried in connection with their part in the Uprising point to both of the other categories of victims and complain that it is the detainees who have been shortchanged. Their argument is that many of those who were injured were simply innocent victims of the violence going on in the city or were reacting to the situation at the time, rather than consciously participating out of commitment to the goals of the Uprising. Yet any survivor who suffered the slightest injury can come forward to claim victim status and compensation, while many among the nonwounded who led the struggle for democracy remain unrecognized.

In addition, many of those who were arrested, tried, and even imprisoned for their leadership roles in the Uprising remained engaged in the democracy movement in Korea throughout the 1980s and into the 1990s and continued their fight against the government. In contrast (the argument goes), the directly affected 5.18 groups have really been progovernment in the sense that they have not been opposed to the government per se but have worked for compensation, and their leaders have acted more as representatives of interest groups in negotiations with the government.

A primary concern of the detained category of victims, then, has been safeguarding the historical interpretation of their actions—in armed resistance against the government—rather than receiving monetary compensation for damages they may have suffered as a result. "Finding out the truth" about 5.18 is important in clearing their names and assuring a place for themselves in the national narrative of patriotic struggle; "keeping the spirit alive" is also a key goal insofar as the values of social justice and democracy for which they fought remain incompletely realized in Korea.

Many of the detained initially refused compensation as a government attempt to "whitewash" the events of May 1980. During the parliamentary investigation of 1988–1989 into 5.18 several Kwangju groups issued a joint statement questioning the government's motives, declaring that "The government authorities' measures to help the bereaved family members of the victims and wounded in the incident, before probing into the truth of the incident, is but a scheme aimed at obliterating the spirit of May" (*Tonga ilbo,* June 21,1988). Later, in a December 14, 1988, statement, Chairman Yun Kang-ok of the 5.18 Kwangju People's Uprising Friendship Association (an association of the detained) put it more bluntly: "We totally reject the legislation of a special law and compensation without ascertaining the truth of the Kwangju Uprising . . . We can hardly suppress our astonishment at reports that the government has earmarked W100 billion to compensate the bereaved family members of the victims who died during the uprising. . . . Talking about compensation without knowing the true picture of the uprising or who was responsible for it is a cunning trick intended to perpetuate another brutal massacre" (cited in *Chosŏn ilbo,* December 15, 1988).

It was only during the second compensation period, in 1993 under President Kim Young Sam, that those who had been arrested were offered money. At that time Yun himself and other holdouts among the detained finally accepted compensation, but they (and other victims) used the money to form the 5.18 Memorial Foundation (see below).[30]

Indicative perhaps of the difference between the attitude of the detained and other victims' groups is the issue of the May protest songs, such as "A March for My Beloved" (see above).[31] This song is said to be about Yun Sang-wŏn, who died on May 27 defending the Provincial Office Building, and his like-minded classmate, Pak Ki-sun.[32] Pak died two years later of *yonton* gas poisoning and was buried separately, but they were later united in a posthumous marriage and lie together in the new 5.18 Cemetery, sharing a grave and headstone. The song's lyrics celebrate self-sacrifice and continuous struggle; like other familiar, militant 5.18 protest tunes, it was normally played and sung all over town in May. In 1998, however, leaders of the commemoration events had begun to disavow the "antigovernment struggle style" characteristic of past anniversaries; in the wake of Kim Dae Jung's election as president, the songs were deemed inappropriate and disappeared.

The notable exception seemed to be at the display in Sangmu New Town sponsored by the AD, where loudspeakers continued to spew forth the familiar melodies. When questioned about why only their group was playing 5.18 songs, members replied that as they had actually done the fighting in 1980, for them these songs had special meaning and thus they (in contrast to others) were unwilling to go along with the popular consensus and give them up.

The Uprising as Civic Asset

New Citizens' Groups and the Reimaging of Kwangju

IN MAY 2000 THE CITY GOVERNMENT moved the Kwangju Biennale, an ambitious biannual, international, progressive/alternative art festival begun in 1995, from the fall to the spring to overlap with the May anniversary events; thus the major civic festivals representing the two sides of Kwangju's self-proclaimed identity—as "City of Arts and Culture" and "Mecca of Democracy"—were joined, creating a single tourist attraction.[1] That year, shuttle buses ran between the 5.18 Cemetery and the Biennale site, and discount admission tickets to the artfest were on sale at a small kiosk near the cemetery entrance. Posters and T-shirts with the slogan "Millenium [*sic*] Long Glow—5.18" (Ch'ŏnnyŏn ŭi Pit 5.18) and depictions of the new Kwangju Uprising "mascot"—Nuxee—appeared on the streets alongside banners proclaiming more traditional sentiments, such as "Let's keep the May spirit alive and drive out the American bastards!" (5 wŏl chŏngsin kyesŭng hayŏ, miguk nomdŭl moranaeja!). This reimaging of Kwangju reflects, in part, the impact of new actors and groups in civic affairs.

Every year the 5.18 anniversary celebration is managed by an anniversary events committee (*haengsa wiwŏn hoe*); the committee chairman (*wiwŏnjang*)—a position of symbolic importance in the 5.18 movement—is selected in the early spring by members of 5.18-related groups, who sponsor the events. By 1995 the sponsoring groups included not just the direct victims' associations (as well as the local and

135

May 17, 2000, Uprising Eve Parade introduces 5.18 cartoon mascot, Nuxee.

provincial governments), but also other new civic organizations with their own agendas. In fact, the chairman that year, a Catholic priest, was himself the head of one such recently established citizens' group, the 5.18 Memorial Foundation—a demonstration of the growing power of these new associations.[2]

The 5.18 Memorial Foundation was started in 1994 with compensation money donated by victims, as well as membership fees from the associated groups. It also receives public funds, which it then can channel into various civic projects (like the anniversary celebration itself); indeed, it was intended to provide a conduit for the flow of money into commemorative activities. Its board of directors included (in 1996) several dozen members representing a broad spectrum of community (as well as 5.18) leaders.

As the chairman of the foundation's board explained to me, "The reason for creating the 5.18 foundation was . . . that there are many groups [*tanch'e*]. While there are points of agreement and joint efforts [among them], there are also many instances when that isn't the case. So we organized the foundation in order that all the groups together become members of the 5.18 foundation and join together to do things. Now there are only one or two groups that don't belong.

There are members of those groups who do, but those groups themselves don't send representatives" (personal communication, 1996). It was the hope that this foundation would provide the momentum for bringing the separate associations together in the future; indeed, one of its primary goals was to unify the different groups and to prevent what was (in the eyes of some observers) the selfish divisiveness of the various factions from presenting a bad image of the 5.18 movement to the public.

Another prominent founding member of the foundation, himself a direct victim who had remained in the Provincial Office Building until the end on May 27 and who had donated his compensation money to the foundation, was more candid in his assessment: "Regardless of the existence of this foundation, it is time for both direct and indirect [other civic] groups to have mutual understanding. When the direct victims' groups were suffering, the civic leaders and so forth didn't care. They just turned their backs. But now the indirect groups have a strong voice. The direct victims' groups see this as nonsense—they think 'after all, you guys didn't suffer and now you are using this opportunity for your own goals.' But now is the time for both sides to have mutual understanding, and understand each other. This is my own choice for the direct victims' groups. If not, the direct victims' groups will have no place in the future" (personal communication, 1996).

In addition to bringing unity to the 5.18 movement, the mission of the foundation is to develop and maintain the Kwangju spirit through the promotion of social, cultural, and research activities—although in reality in the mid-1990s the group had very little money with which to work, since anticipated funding from the central government had not yet materialized.[3]

Another of the ascendant new citizens' groups in Kwangju that is connected to the memorialization of 5.18 is Kwangju Citizens' Solidarity (Kwangju Simin Yŏndae Moim—KCS). KCS was started in 1993 when a loose coalition of citizens' groups and concerned individuals joined together in opposition to plans for the construction of a large 5.18 monument. It was not that the members were against the building of monuments per se. In fact, in 1994 the group was active in the campaign to build a tower of stones at the Mangwŏl-dong cemetery and in the movement to preserve the Sangmudae prison and courtroom as historical sites. Rather, they were citizens who simply were seeking a role in the decision-making process. The group functioned so well that members decided to continue working together to have a voice in 5.18-related civic affairs.

Thirteen citizens' groups came together to formally found the original organization; in late 1994 it was reestablished as an independent organization with individual members. It remains by design a rather small association, composed of a core group of fewer than fifty like-minded individuals, almost all professionals (lawyers, doctors, college professors, and journalists) (KCS 1996a). Unlike the 5.18 Memorial Foundation, which explicitly seeks to be a coalition of direct victims and civic leaders, very few of the KCS members are themselves Uprising survivors. The ones who are were college students or professors at the time and are in the category of people who were detained and/or arrested.

As a group, KCS is deeply concerned with overcoming the problem of the isolation of Kwangju and the surrounding Honam region. Its strategy is the promotion of the globalization of the "Kwangju spirit" through education about 5.18 and the forging of links with the international human rights community, particularly among Korea's Asian neighbors. Accordingly, KCS's efforts during the annual anniversary celebrations have focused on academic conferences and symposia that bring foreigners to Kwangju to share in the commemoration of 5.18 and to learn from its example. KCS literature envisions Kwangju as a "Mecca of Democracy" comparable to the Paris Commune and Auschwitz; Kwangju's "solemn struggle for democracy has moved the hearts of people across the world who have truly loved peace and freedom," and "People will remember Kwangju forever as a torch for freedom, peace, and equality, which are universal virtues of mankind" (KCS 1995:2). By capitalizing on Kwangju's legitimacy as the symbolic center of the now successful Korean democracy movement and promoting the continuing vitality of the "Kwangju spirit," KCS seeks to transform what remains, from the perspective of other 5.18 groups, a local/regional tragedy and national "problem" into a civic asset, utilizing the events of May to advance a new image of the city. This vision of the legacy of 5.18 emphasizes Kwangju's ongoing importance as a national and international role model, rather than as a site of remembered suffering and resistance.

Thus in May 1995 KCS held an international symposium on "Inhumane Acts and Their Resolution," which included as panelists representatives from the Argentinian human rights group Mothers for the May Plaza Victims (See introduction). A more ambitious project in May 1996 brought together from Korea and over twenty other countries almost one hundred college students and young adults active in human rights organizations for a six-day First International Youth Camp for Human Rights and Peace. As the project's rationale explained:

> In May 1980 ordinary citizens and students of Kwangju rose up against the military dictatorship, demanding the creation of a democratic government and observance of human rights. . . . Based on this Kwangju spirit, we've kept moving against all the obstacles of democracy in the last 16 years. It hasn't been easy. . . . Over the past decade, South Korea has made dramatic strides in the arena of international business and technological advancement. However, the struggle for full democracy, human rights, and social justice continues to lag behind this economic prosperity. We've observed that similar situations exist in other countries in Asia and around the world. For that reason, we invite people of good will, especially the youth and students who will carry the burden of this continuing struggle in the future, to join us in Kwangju to share experiences and reflections on our common task of making a better society for all (KCS 1996b:16–17).

Participants attended the major 5.18 anniversary events in Kwangju and met together in sessions to share "concrete information on the exploitation and oppression of people in undemocratic societies" (KCS 1996b:17).

On the eighteenth anniversary in 1998, KCS organized a conference jointly with the Asian Human Rights Commission (Hong Kong), at which Asian human rights activists gathered in Kwangju to declare the newly drafted Asian Human Rights Charter.[4]

In proclaiming the importance of Kwangju as a venue for the declaration of this charter, KCS stated that

> the Kwangju Massacre stands symbolic of the failure of almost all the Asian countries to develop meaningful democracy during the 20th century. However, the determination of those who faced the massacre

and gave their lives and the determination of the people of Kwangju City to defend the honor of those who died and to keep the flame of solidarity alive and further the continuous influence of the Kwangju Massacre in the political life of South Korea as a whole is symbolic of the aspirations of the people to part from repression and militarism and to seek an altered world where human life is respected. . . . The spirit of the Asian Human Rights Charter too is the same for all the people of Asia. In this sense having the declaration of the Asian Human Rights Charter in Kwangju has a very comprehensive meaning (KCS 1998).

By linking the determination of those who actually participated in the Kwangju Uprising (and even died in 1980) with the determination of the ordinary citizens of Kwangju, who have worked since then to redeem the national reputation of their city, KCS asserts the right of everyone—not just those who were direct victims of the Uprising—to lay claim to the legacy of 5.18 and the moral legitimacy its heritage now bestows. All Kwangju citizens are its rightful heirs—and perhaps all Koreans, too, who have worked for democracy and social justice. This broader, more symbolic interpretation of the "Kwangju spirit" empowers all Kwangju citizens and at the same time dilutes the privileged status of the direct victims' groups and weakens their a priori claims to civic leadership roles.

In fact, KCS members consciously seek to distance themselves from the direct victims' groups, whom they consider to be too "emotional" in their representations of the Kwangju Uprising. They express the idea that the overly hysterical and impassioned tone of victims' testimony is counterproductive; their rhetoric makes outsiders uncomfortable, and they come across as too biased to be effective spokespeople for Kwangju.

In contrast, KCS actively promotes accounts that appear more disinterested and nonpartisan, particularly the testimony of non-Koreans. In 1997, the KCS anniversary project was the publication of the personal recollections of foreign correspondents who had covered the Kwangju Uprising. At a press conference in Kwangju on May 17 celebrating the publication of *Kwangju in the Eyes of the World* (KCS 1997), attended by most of those who had contributed essays to the volume, the chairman of *Mudŭng ilbo*,[5] said that the book, which appeared in both Korean and English versions, excluded Kwangju residents not only to make the events of May 1980 more accessible to the outside world, but also to make the volume more objective. As the preface to the book asserts, "In the search for truth, objectivity is always deemed the prerequisite. History, like science, demands an unimpassioned observer to chronicle its events. It hopes that from his unbiased vantage point, this onlooker will be able to balance the scales, absorb the circumstances, intentions, motivations, and consequences, and come out with a story that tells the whole tale. Thus the modern world has chosen the foreign correspondent as its historian—hoping that his eyes, unmoved by patriotism or ideologic concerns, will not be blinded; praying that his story, unfettered by censorship or national security concerns, will be related in its entirety" (KCS 1997). The foreign reporter is "the voice that shall be believed" (KCS 1997:x); implicitly, the voices of the victims themselves are inherently "unobjective" and thus less believable, inevitably tainted by personal and ideological concerns.

In addition, KCS opposes the contentious attitude of the direct victims' groups. One member in 1996 cited, as an example of the continuing oppositional priorities of other Kwangju groups, the efforts of a prominent 5.18 activist to put on trial not only the leaders of the Kwangju Massacre, but also the soldiers who had done the killing—a campaign KCS members did not support (and that did not succeed).[6] This is not to suggest KCS members in the mid-1990s felt that the Kwangju Uprising was "over"; rather, the remaining issues with which they were concerned involved government responsibility and accountability in a symbolic rather than a concrete sense. That is, admissions of guilt and contrition and educating the nation about the facts of 5.18 were more important than punishing individual paratroopers or even giving more money to the victims.

In a scholarly presentation at a KCS-sponsored symposium in 1995 (at the height of the Chun/Roh prosecution drive), the lawyer Pak Wonsoon (1995:33) argued (in a manner reminiscent of the complaints made by some 5.18 victims' groups in the late 1980s) that the government was trying to solve the problem of Kwangju solely through "compensation"—that is, offering comfort money to the victims—rather than "reparations," which would involve the acknowledgment that the government had acted illegally and thus needed to do much more than give monetary restitution to direct victims. Citing a 1994 survey in Kwangju showing that 53 percent of ordinary citizens and 63 percent of civic leaders thought that "finding out the truth" was the most important unresolved issue about 5.18, Pak (1995:18) pointed out that, in light of international standards for reparations, this demand for government honesty was not unreasonable (1995:17; also Pak 2000:251–253); instead, the policy of the Kim Young Sam government treated the "Kwangju problem" (*Kwangju munje*) as a regional event that could be settled quickly through money (1995:15)—an opinion widely shared in Kwangju. Indeed, as we have seen, by the mid-1990s, the victims had been awarded compensation in a series of government acts. One hundred *p'yong* of the former army base, Sangmudae, was given to the people of Kwangju as collective restitution, and in 1997 the expensive new 5.18 Cemetery was completed.[7]

In the eyes of most Kwangju citizens, then, the 5.18 victims' associations had by the late 1990s benefited sufficiently from the government's largesse, and public sympathy for them had run its course. Any further claims or demands are seen as selfish and greedy, and concrete proposals that address these groups' specific needs are thought of as narrowly self-serving. As one KCS member explained, what separates the various 5.18 associations is self-interest: "When the groups were struggling for compensation, others could sympathize with them. But now, most Kwangju people are fed up with the 5.18 groups. Even more, people outside Kwangju are fed up with them. . . . To lead the 5.18 movement, they should have a high level of morality, but these groups have lost their legitimacy. . . . through the compensation and cemetery, they [in this case, the bereaved families' association] have money and [a] good position—but they just fight among themselves for relative power within the organization. Some people are good, but others are not" (personal communication, 1996).

In contrast, KCS envisions its projects as serving a public, rather than private, interest. KCS has been able to mobilize resources beyond the Korean Peninsula. Its projects have required money, English-language ability, global connections, and the sophistication to conceive of them in the first place. There are KCS members who have traveled overseas, lived in the United States, and/or have significant networks and ties (through occupation, family, or educational experiences) that extend well beyond Honam. The group has proven skillful

[margin handwriting: victims' groups getting greedy?]

at raising funds for its projects; it has a website; it has formed an English-study circle. KCS has internationalized its efforts in ways significantly beyond the means of other 5.18-related groups in Kwangju.

Yet it could be argued that the KCS's is still a transnational project with a remarkably local agenda: a bigger role in city affairs, a larger voice in the future direction of Kwangju's development, the boosting of civic pride, and ultimately the rehabilitation and en-hancement of Kwangju's (and the Honam region's) image within the nation. While bringing interested groups to Kwangju educates for-eigners about 5.18 and spreads the "Kwangju spirit," the impetus for these projects is clearly also the impact they have had on KCS prestige and power within the local community.

power, prestige and $, who is above all this? (not many)

What Is the "Kwangju Spirit"?

THE GROWING INFLUENCE OF THE NEW civic groups in Kwangju is dependent, as has been suggested, on a more symbolic and inclusive interpretation of the meaning of the Kwangju Uprising and its "spirit" and the presumption that all Kwangju citizens—and even perhaps all Koreans—are rightful heirs to its legacy. Not surprisingly (as we have also seen), the directly affected groups have supported a narrower, more concrete and practical construction of the Uprising's meaning and their own privileged claims to it. A 1988 survey that compared the attitudes of direct victims with the general Kwangju citizenry found that direct victims were more likely to regard themselves or the people of the Honam region, and not Koreans in general, as the victims of 5.18. They also were more inclined to see responsibility for its resolution as belonging to them rather than to the nation as a whole (PJC 1988:61).

At this point we might ask, To what extent can all Kwangju citizens lay claim to 5.18? It is true that there was support from every stratum of society within Kwangju during May 1980 for the events taking place downtown, and citizens participated in many ways: giving food and money, demonstrating, and helping to maintain the peaceful atmosphere that prevailed during the days of "Free Kwangju." Students were the "trigger" that started the demonstrations in the first days, and intellectuals and civic and religious leaders labored toward the end to resolve the conflict through the work of the Incident Settlement Com-

144

mittee. Even for those less directly involved, the Uprising touched the lives of most of Kwangju's citizens. The majority witnessed some sort of violence or evidence thereof, and significant numbers joined in the demonstrations or at least went out to look (PJC 1988:24–28). However, conceptualizing the Kwangju Uprising as an event resulting from overwhelming popular support and participation and the 5.18 movement itself as a broad-based citizens' movement, an umbrella under which all Kwangjuites can stand, suppresses such issues as social class and other divisions within the city in 1980 and serves to devalue the disproportional suffering—and thus the need for special attention—of those directly affected.

It is an inescapable fact that the majority of the victims were lower class; as noted, about 70 percent of those who died were working class or unemployed, and evidence suggests the same is true for the injured and arrested. Less than one-third were students. However, it was common in the 1990s to tout the participation of lower-class people in the events of May as an indication of the inclusive, communal spirit that the Uprising engendered—"Even prostitutes gave blood" is a favorite example—rather than to identify them as the segment of the population that made the rebellion.[1] The political scientist Sonn Ho-ch'ŏl, in his analysis of 5.18 from the perspective of class, quotes an unemployed worker who pointed out that the rich people in the neighborhood behind the Provincial Office Building all ran away while many orphans and others with pitiful lives participated. Sonn comments that the worker's analysis shows more insight than the social scientists' and suggests that civic leaders who urged *simin'gun* to turn in their guns could be viewed as opponents, rather than supporters, of the uprising (Sonn 1995:173).

As has already been mentioned, a 1988 public opinion survey in Kwangju found that the majority of ordinary citizens were largely unaware of the efforts of the Incident Settlement Committee. Of the respondents, 34 percent had never heard of the committee and 31.4 percent knew of it but were not sure about its exact role (PJC 1988:30). Further, in response to questions about the committee's efforts, only about 20 percent evaluated its activities favorably; more than 50 percent felt the group had done badly or only "so-so" (PJC 1988:31).

Often conveniently forgotten, as well, are images of civic leaders being booed off the platform at the mass rally on May 22 by crowds of angry citizens dissatisfied with their negotiations with the military on behalf of the city (see Hwang Sŏk Yŏng 1985:144–146) and the accounts of factory owners who tried to prevent their workers from participating (Sonn 1995:173–174). There were also the well-known debates about whether to turn in the guns or continue to fight, as well as the splits within both the rebel and civic leadership (see Hwang Sŏk Yŏng 1985:183–197; KCSPRI 1991:33–36)—disputes and ruptures that linger even today in divisions within 5.18 movement groups (see AD 1997:10–13).

Nothing epitomizes these differences so well perhaps as the recollections of Cho A-ra, then the director of the YWCA. Cho, who was known in the region as the "Mother of Democracy" (KCSPRI 1991:40), participated in the Incident Settlement Committee's efforts to persuade the *simin'gun* to turn in their guns. On the final evening before the government troops returned, Cho and other civic and religious leaders listened to the rebels in the Provincial Office Building declare their intention of remaining to the end, even if it meant death. Her description of the evening ends simply with her memory that "It was 7 P.M. At about 8, I said, 'Let's go home.' I went out with Fr. Cho Bi-oh and Prof. Oh Byŏng-mun, who accompanied me as far as the YWCA. That evening, too, I walked home with Lee Ch'ong-mu." She awoke the next morning to gunfire, tanks in the streets, and bullet holes in the YWCA (KMHRI 1990:139).

This is quite a different story from the one told in the official Kwangju City government account of *The May 18 Kwangju Democratic Uprising,* in which, almost twenty years later, the lines among different degrees and kinds of popular participation have been completely erased. In outlining the "meanings" of 5.18 and the "truth" of the uprising as "Kwangju citizens experienced [it] in person," the official account makes everyone a hero: "Almost all the citizens voluntarily fought in the face of the cruel violence of the paratroopers. Considering the situation, it was impossible to participate in the uprising unless one was ready to risk all things, including life. Nevertheless, the Kwangju citizens resisted injustice in one body in the name of all Korean citizens, so it was not just one or two individuals' heroic uprising, but a whole people resisting oppression, and it brought them a glorious victory in the end" (Kwangju City, 5.18 Historiographic Committee 1998:173).

As should be obvious, the special status of the direct victims' groups is inevitably diminished and their character obscured as the categories of "victim" and "participant" are more generally and less literally defined and as others who have been active in the more far-reaching Korean democracy movement can lay claim to those roles. From this broader perspective, within Kwangju all citizens have legitimacy in the 5.18 movement. On a national level, as the Kwangju Uprising has been appropriated in the 1980s by the students, intellectuals, academics, social activists, and other citizens who participated in the struggle for democracy during the Fifth Republic, all those who fought for social reforms during the 1980s—and by extension in the 1960s and 1970s as well—are linked as comrades-in-arms with those who died in Kwangju.

In 1995 one event held in conjunction with the fifteenth anniversary was an international conference on "A Scientific Approach to the May Uprising in Kwangju." One academic who was presenting a paper, a Korean scholar who teaches in the United States, was challenged by a member of the audience. "What gives you the right," the local man asked, "to discuss the Kwangju Uprising? You weren't there; how do you think you can talk about it?" The scholar's response articulated very well this appropriating process; in legitimating his claim to 5.18, the scholar replied that he too had been a student demonstrator in the 1960s and so had known the experiences and aspirations of the students in Kwangju. In May 1980 Kwangju citizens had been acting on shared ideals and goals with common roots in the (larger) Korean student movement.

The hegemonic view of the successful 1987 Korean prodemocracy movement is that the achievement of a democratic government was made possible by wide popular support, particularly from the middle class.[2] Thus it is not surprising that as the Kwangju Uprising has become situated within the decades-long national democratization struggle, the dominant interpretation of 5.18 retrospectively too could become a broad-based citizens' movement—making it possible for more of Kwangju's citizens, and no longer just direct victims and survivors, to contend for civic leadership roles via the 5.18 movement.

What, then, is the "Kwangju spirit"? The "Kwangju spirit" (and "reviving," "renewing," or "keeping it alive") is the banner under which, it appears, the 5.18 movement will march into the next century.

Yet its meaning has changed a great deal over the past two decades, particularly for those who hold an inclusive view of 5.18 as signifying a broad-based civic movement.

Prior to the establishment of civilian rule (with the election of Kim Young Sam) in 1993, the "Kwangju spirit" was a more specific, less contested notion. Quite simply, it was invariably evoked in local, national, and even international arenas in support of the achievement of a democratic government. For example, a *Han'gyŏrye shinmun* editorial on the occasion of the twelfth anniversary of 5.18 criticized the national and democratic circles, as well as the opposition party, for failing "to realize the spirit of the Kwangju Uprising, even though more than 10 years have passed since that tragic incident." In the future, the editors opined, "we firmly believe that the spirit of the Kwangju Uprising will be brilliantly revived if all democratic forces centering around the Democratic Party firmly unite to achieve a grand democratic alliance and marched toward the establishment of a democratic government" (May 20, 1992). International human rights groups and concerned Western academics, too, pointed to Kwangju as "evidence of strong drives and passions for democracy in Korea" (Cumings 1984:1). And in Kwangju itself the different constituent elements of the 5.18 movement united and aligned with other national groups under the democracy movement banner.

Frequently linked with democracy in the 1980s was the additional goal of autonomy, or independence, in the sense of freedom from interference by outside powers (specifically the United States). It was these two purposes, *minju hwa* (democratization) and *chaju hwa* (autonomy) that were cited by the 5.18 victims' groups as the meanings inherent in the "Kwangju spirit" (PJC 1988:51). Indeed, in the Chun era the Kwangju Uprising came to symbolize growing anti-American sentiment almost as much as it did Koreans' democratic aspirations.[3] As Cumings notes, "The radical tendencies of the 1980s . . . deepened the anti-Americanism that many Koreans had felt all along, but especially after the Kwangju Rebellion. Radicals linked Korea's internal repression to the history of American imperialism in Korea and elsewhere and thus drew upon deep well-springs of nationalism. Kwangju brought all this to a head" (1997:382). In short, to understand dissent (particularly student protests) in the 1980s, "The touchstone was always Kwangju and the American reaction to it" (Cumings 1997:384).

Much of the anti-American activism in the 1980s (especially by students) directly claimed U.S. actions during and after May 1980 as a motive. The leader of the group of dissenters who set fire to the USIS Cultural Center in Pusan in 1982 cited the role of the United States as "a patron of dictatorial political power" in Kwangju as a reason; students who occupied the USIS Cultural Center in Seoul in 1985 demanded a public apology from U.S. officials for their complicity in 1980 (Lee Samsung 1988:72).

In Kwangju the ACC was burned in 1980 and was attacked so many times (twenty-six in all)[4] that by 1988 it was forced to close, then relocate. A *Chŏnnam ilbo* telephone poll taken after a 1989 rally in Kwangju to abolish the ACC found 40 percent in favor of closure and only 22.9 percent who wanted it to remain open; 86.8 percent cited U.S. support for Chun in May 1980 as the reason for their negative feelings, and 90.5 percent agreed that the United States was obstructing democratization in Korea (*Chŏnnam ilbo*, February 7, 1989). The new center, heavily fortified, reopened in June 1990 and suffered eighty attacks in the next three years;[5] it remained a target for anti-American activism in Kwangju until it was finally closed in 1998.

These two meanings of the "Kwangju spirit"—democracy and independence—were linked to the events of May 1980 through the actions of the citizens and the *simin'gun* at both ends of the Uprising, when people took up arms to oppose the military dictatorship. It was the willingness of so many in Kwangju to struggle against oppression that was celebrated; in particular, the bravery of those who made a last stand on May 27 at the Provincial Office Building, even when there was a high probability of failure, was often invoked as a shining example of what could be achieved when humans were willing to stand up to tyranny and persecution. It is this final night that best represented the essence of 5.18.

This 1980s perspective emphasized the actions of those who fought, their heroism and self-sacrifice, as much as the values for which they struggled as the most important aspect of the "Kwangju spirit." By the 1990s, however, this focus had begun to shift away from the valor of the victims (away even from who they specifically were, as we have seen) to connect the "Kwangju spirit" with the much broader, more nebulous goal of human rights. By standing against the military government, Kwangju's citizens were defending human dignity; human rights are about violations of human dignity by any kind of oppressive power. Thus the "Kwangju spirit" began to be transformed from the struggle for democracy and independence in Korea into a generalized concern for global human rights.

With this new interpretation, the meaning of the "Kwangju spirit" has finally been cut loose from its historical contingencies and the particular circumstances in Korea in 1980 that gave rise to the event. Decontextualized, it can be reimaged in more comfortable ways disconnected from 1990s manifestations of lingering 1980s social issues. Kwangju civic groups can now conjure up the "Kwangju spirit" in discussions of democracy in Southeast Asia but conveniently forget its relevance to problems with socioeconomic cleavages at home.

In conjunction with this broadening of the meaning of 5.18, there has also been a change in focus from the two ends of the Uprising to the middle (so to speak)—i.e., to the interlude now dubbed "Free Kwangju." People in Kwangju have always taken pride in the orderly and peaceful way life went on in the days between May 21 (when the army was driven to the edge of the city) and May 27 (when soldiers returned to take it back). Despite the suspension of the operation of normal official systems of social control, chaos did not prevail; there was no looting or violence, and citizens worked together to cope with the crisis in an atmosphere of cooperation and mutual support.

In the 1980s, Kwangju citizens pointed to the period of "Free Kwangju" in arguing that the government's characterization of the Uprising as a "mob action" or "riot," for the duration of which most decent people hid in their homes in terror, was a distortion and a slanderous misrepresentation of both the spirit and the truth of 5.18. By the 1990s, however, the interlude of "Free Kwangju" was discussed not just in counterpoint to government propaganda, but also as the embodiment of the core meaning of the "Kwangju spirit." During that period, citizens "gave full play to their moral consciousness" (Kwangju City, 5.18 Historiographic Committee 1998:174) and realized (if only briefly) their goals of democracy and community. Those in Kwangju overcame the divisions within the city at the time to work together. In this way, 5.18 serves as an example for overcoming Korean national divisions as well, not just in the sense of regional splits, but also the larger goal of reunification.

To those who hold an inclusive view of 5.18, then, as a broad-

based civil uprising, its essence is now not resistance, the willingness
to fight to the end, as embodied in the heroic struggle of those who
died. Rather, it is something shared by the majority of Kwangju citizens, who participated in the days of "Free Kwangju." The real meaning of the "Kwangju spirit" and the important part of 5.18 is the
cooperative feeling that prevailed during those days and the successful creation of a "model" democratic society in that short time before
the army retook the city. Civic solidarity is sought and celebrated in
this common accomplishment of 5.18 and the shared aspiration for
democracy. Left unexamined is the more problematic issue of divisions within the city during the days of "Free Kwangju" over how best
that dream could be achieved: fighting to the end versus turning in
the guns and seeking a peaceful resolution with the military regime. It
is easy to forget twenty years later that this was an issue in which
some (and only some) of Kwangju's citizens voted with their lives.

division, even during "free Kwangju"

Remembering Kwangju in Post-*Minjung* Korea

*Don't come to my grave if our country is under the heel of the
American bastards;*
Don't come to my grave if our people are living torn apart in two;
*May, like that day, fight on, on the battleground we have passed on
to you;*
Don't come to my grave if our people are living torn apart in two.

*Come to my grave when, exhausted by the long fight, you are falling
down;*
Come to my grave, and I will fill you with my unused passion.
*May, on that road, the red blood and blue dreams of 19 year olds,
completely spilled.*[1]
Come to my grave, and I will fill you with my unused passion.

Come to my grave and play on the day when we finally win.
Come to my grave and play when the flag of our free country waves.
*May, like that day, when the whole world is decorated with taedong
flowers*[2]
Come to my grave and play when the flag of our free country waves.
                    —From "A Dying Wish," a popular May protest song

Now, as an unhappy era has been brought to a close and history is victorious, 5.18 is approaching a second stage, changing to a spirit of universal humanity. Accordingly, the underlying tone of the commemoration events must be stripped of the so-called antigovernment struggle style of the past.

                              —Chŏng Su-man, BFA chairman[3]

IT WOULD BE IRONIC IF THE PRICE of the restoration of Kwangju's honor, the result of state appropriation of 5.18 and the consequent national recognition and memorialization of May, is the erasure from public memory of the long struggle to realize that goal and the continued suffering of many of its victims. As the Kwangju Uprising story is retold in stone at the monumental new 5.18 Cemetery, its end point frozen in time on May 27, 1980, the Uprising's postlude plays on. There are in Kwangju many whose personal histories are counterhegemonic, whose very bodies even offer a site for resistance to the imposition of a singular 5.18 narrative and the amnesia of commemoration in the late 1990s. "History has a problematic relationship to the lived body of the individual who participated in it; in fact it operates more efficiently when survivors are no longer alive" (Sturken 1991:132)—or perhaps when they are effectively silenced.

In the changing political context of the post-*minjung* era in Korea, it may be that Kwangju's survivors (as has been suggested) lack the skills and resources to successfully compete in an emergent civil society in which new social groups now seek to express and advance their own influence and aims and where attention to particularistic concerns risks the charge of petty self-interest. As Kim Sunhyuk points out, "Labeling some issues as trivial and instead imposing 'greater' goals is merely the mirror image of the authoritarian past to which South Korea does not want to regress" (1996:95). In the case of the 5.18 groups in Kwangju, the new emphasis in the late 1990s on the "greater" goal of international human rights to the exclusion of more specific, private, and individual agendas (such as adequate medical care for the injured) represents an autocratic appropriation of the "Kwangju spirit." And to deny victims a voice is to revictimize them as well.

[margin handwritten note: departure from specific agendas to int'l agendas]

Unfortunately, interpretations of the "Kwangju spririt" at the turn of the century point to the imposition of just such lofty visions. In the words of the chairman of the Seventeenth Anniversary Committee, "It is not to remember the painful past, but to prepare for a new future" (AEC 1997a:1). Or as a recent Kwangju City government-sponsored account of the Kwangju Uprising grandly concludes, "All the nation as well as citizens should embrace the spirit of the May 18 Kwangju Democratic Uprising and prepare for the future, rather than sticking to the past. . . . We must realize our community and our history, and let go of the pain and distress of the past. Through the realization of our community which helps and trusts each other and lives and lets lives, the spirit of the Kwangju Democratic Uprising should shine brightly into tomorrow" (Kwangju City, 5.18 Historiographic Committee 1998:179).

But which citizens, exactly, are to let go of the "pain and distress of the past"? Obviously public neglect of the very real physical, social, and psychological problems many survivors in Kwangju continue to face serves to marginalize them further and stands in contradiction to the vision of "community" the "Kwangju spirit" is said to embody. Indeed, it would seem the promotion of "human dignity" surely should extend to a renewed civic concern for the quality of the lives of 5.18 victims and for such related issues as the treatment of the disabled in Korea.[4] It should speak to socioeconomic disparities as well. The class composition of the 5.18-related groups in the 1990s in large part reproduces the original social class divisions existing in Kwangju in 1980 at the time of the Uprising; to the extent that the dead were by and large poorer and less educated than average, so too were their surviving relatives and comrades. Furthermore, as has already been noted, throughout the 1980s the direct victims in general remained poor, with many suffering downward mobility. As Abelmann says of South Korean activism in the 1990s:

> In the case of South Korea, it is not only lives that spill over the divides of changed local and transnational circumstances and idioms, but also persistent social problems. The lives of South Korean farmers, for example, are still very much authored by grand narratives (including internationalization, the free market, neoliberalism, and modernity) and the sites of power—the state, for example—are not enigmatic or dispersed. The consideration of dissent in the late twentieth century demands attention to the heterogeneous nature of the spaces and discourses of dissent—the co-existence of local legacies and idioms with transnational circumstances and the personal rendering of past activisms that live in the face of divergent public memories (1997: 273).

In the government's discourse on the national democratization movement and Kwangju's place in it, citizens are asked to celebrate the achievement of democratization without remembering the *minjung* activism of the 1980s that brought the long process to fruition.

To even name the event is now to forget: the government has rein-scribed it the "5.18 Democratization Movement." In contrast, those in Kwangju continue to use the term "5.18 People's Uprising," (a title that references the struggles of the not so distant past and in which the legacy of the *minjung* movement lingers on).[5] In May, street arches, banners, and signs in Kwangju commemorating the anniversary carry both designations, depending on whether they have been erected by the government, on the one hand, or by 5.18 movement and Kwangju civic organizations, students, labor unions, or other activist groups, on the other.[6]

Yet the trend even in Kwangju (as we have seen) is away from the activism and oppositional political character of past Mays. As the quote at the beginning of this chapter from the BFA chairman sug-gests, in 1997 members of the Anniversary Events Committee called for an end to the "antigovernment struggle style" of memorial events. This was no guarantee that individual groups and organizations would forsake the oppositional tenor of past Mays. After all, as one observer noted (of the seventeenth anniversary), as the various groups concerned with the anniversary do not share a unified point of view and as the memorialization period extends over a full month, the commemoration is an assortment of events put together "department store-style" (*paekhwajŏmsik;* literally "100 goods store").[7]

Still, this declaration was significant in that it is the Anniversary Events Committee that sets the tone for the commemorative activi-ties in any given year. By deciding who will lead the festivities and by establishing an official agenda for the anniversary—agreeing on a slo-gan(s) and goals for the commemoration and approving proposed events—the committee leadership represents a kind of civic consen-sus in Kwangju about the direction of the "5.18 movement" and its (immediate) future.[8] Strategic decisions such as who is elected chair-man of the committee and what the slogan will be reflect the ebb and flow of influence of different groups and follow the weight of local public opinion in negotiating the faultlines of national political dis-course. In recent years the chairmen have been prominent profession-als (a priest, a college professor, and a lawyer) whose revolutionary credentials derive from their roles on the Incident Settlement Com-mittee. The slogans have moved from concrete, 5.18-based activist de-mands such as "Prosecute the Murderers!" (in 1995, in the midst of a

specific demands ⇩ *vague generalities*

national campaign to do so) through the familiar *minjung* refrains of "The Rebirth of May! Autonomy, Democracy, Reunification" (in 1996, when the outcome of the trial was still unclear) to the vague generalities of "Human Rights and Peace, for a Harmonious Future" (in 1998, after the election of Kim Dae Jung).

In 1998 as well (as has been mentioned), the informal proscription of 5.18 songs was by and large successful. The lyrics of most of the "May songs" celebrate not just the Kwangju Uprising itself, but also its connections to struggle and resistance to any form of imperialism, and for this reason the popular tunes are problematic. The words of "A Dying Wish" (at the beginning of this chapter), for example, typify the linkage in *minjung* discourse of 5.18 with the continuing movement for decolonization, represented by the achievement of reunification (see Choi Chungmoo 1995: 105-106). In this song, the image of the Kwangju martyrs is conjured not in service to the international capitalist system (as in the prime minister's exhortations presented above) but as an inspiration in the fight against U.S. domination and national division. As Wells notes, "The minjung issue is a struggle over legitimacy, and the articulators of minjung ideology—or ideologies—consciously and often vehemently represent to the Korean people two stark choices: leadership of and by the minjung into a new era of reunification as a genuine Korean nation; or perpetuation of an alien system of politics that makes the continuing tragic division of the nation the cornerstone of power" (1995a:17).

Given the common assumption that to embrace the *minjung* movement is to reject the South Korean government as illegitimate, it is easy to understand why Kwangju's civic leaders would wish, in the newly dawned era of the Kim Dae Jung regime, to minimize the use of *minjung* imagery in the anniversary events. Thus in the May 1998 Uprising Eve Fest the annual retelling of the Kwangju Uprising story was presented in the form of an extended montage of film footage of 5.18 projected on the large screen above the stage on the Provincial Office Building plaza—and the images were shown not to the accompaniment of the May songs, but to the "Last of the Mohicans" soundtrack.[9]

In addition to groups in Kwangju, the Anniversary Events Committee has also had to deal in May with the role of other national social movements that have historically claimed 5.18 as part of their own *minjung* struggle narrative and thus have played an active part in the Upris-

Student activists in Uprising Eve Parade, May 17, 1996.

ing anniversary. Two of these, the student movement and the democratic labor movement, remained a presence in Kwangju in May in the
late 1990s, although their public reception has been quite different.

As late as 1996, college students were highly visible participants
in the Uprising anniversary festivities. That year, hundreds of students
marched in the Uprising Eve Parade (on May 17) and held rallies night
after night on the blocked off main thoroughfare, Kŭmnamno, singing
5.18 songs, chanting antigovernment slogans, dancing to *samulnori*
bands, and setting small bonfires in the street. In the words of one
American college student observing the scene, it was a sort of "political
Mardi Gras"—lively and festive but with a militant edge. In 1997, however, there was no Uprising Eve Parade on May 17, and the students
were kept to the margins, pushed out of the official program. Their role
that year was as disrupters rather than as participants, battling riot police
late into the night, every night for a week, in the streets around the Provincial Office Building. Even during the daily graveside memorial events,
riot police generally kept student groups contained in the old cemetery
area, which became the de facto antigovernment/anti-American protest
site and the staging ground for forays into the new cemetery; in one incident on May 18, a group of about two hundred militant students

charged the main altar and attempted to tear down the memorial wreaths sent by government officials. However, the students were repulsed by a dozen bereaved family members who, quickly mobilizing from the various grave sites where they had been holding private family rites, confronted the students and, angrily berating them, tried to chase them away from the central plaza.

Thus by the late 1990s, activist students were no longer welcome, even on the sacred terrain in Kwangju where not so long before, on anniversaries past, they had joined with Kwangju citizens in fighting the riot police. This antistudent stance was a conscious policy on the part of the Anniversary Events Committee. In April 1997, a local university student had died in a demonstration; his body was still in the hospital, and the students wanted to hold a public funeral for him concurrent with the anniversary events. Sentiment in Kwangju, however, was turning against this kind of student activism.[10] With the image of Kwangju improving in the eyes of the nation, civic leaders feared the cooptation of the 5.18 commemoration program by radical students and opposed the continued association of Kwangju with violent antigovernment protests. Even the media were unanimous in condemning the students' plans, and students were denied an official part in the proceedings. So although students (not just from Kwangju but from all over the country) made their presence known—marching about the city, holding noisy rallies, trying almost daily to get to the center of town, and disrupting organized memorial events—public opinion was not sympathetic, and they were unable to muster support for their cause.[11]

If activist students had not attempted to promote their own antigovernment agenda during May in Kwangju or had not been so intransigent in the face of popular disenchantment with their tactics, perhaps they could have continued to have an important role in the commemoration events. Student unwillingness to comply with the "new," less confrontational, unprovocative, peaceful—essentially depoliticized— tone of the anniversary events espoused by Kwangju's civic leaders in the late 1990s caused their displacement to the margins.

Obviously, this mirrors the situation on the larger national scene, where the student movement had in the late 1990s become more radical and less influential. Particularly in the wake of the Yonsei University incident of August 1996 and the government's subsequent

successful efforts to stigmatize Hanch'ongnyŏn, the National Federation of Student Councils, as antistate, the student movement was by
May 1997 more isolated;[12] even Kwangju's tolerant and long-suffering
citizenry could finally say "enough."[13]

In contrast to the students, another waning national social
movement with a claim to the symbolic capital of the Kwangju Uprising, the labor movement, has been more successful in maintaining its
stake in the anniversary commemoration and using the May events to
advance its political agenda in post-*minjung* Korea.[14] In 1997, the
same May the students were banished, democratic labor (*minju
noch'ong*) successfully inaugurated the National Democratic Taxi
Drivers' Federated Union in Kwangju. In an event that brought together national and local democratic labor leaders, Anniversary
Events Committee members, 5.18 survivors, and taxi drivers from
around the country, the role of taxi drivers (and by extension all laborers) in the Kwangju Uprising was remembered and extolled, and
the establishment of the new union was celebrated.

May 20 is customarily set aside in Kwangju as "Democratic Drivers' Day" (as noted above) in recognition of the decisive role played
by drivers at this point in the Uprising, and in 1997 the commemorative event included a reenactment of the vehicle demonstration.[15]
Following a sound truck carrying Kwangju dignitaries and labor leaders, a parade of about one thousand drivers—on foot, in a line of almost one hundred taxis, four abreast, or riding in the buses in which
they had come from other parts of the country—proceeded downtown to the Provincial Office Building, where, in a brief ceremony,
labor protest songs were sung and a statement was read honoring
Kwangju's "democratic drivers" and proclaiming the goals of the new
labor union.[16] Tying the union's inauguration with the commemoration of 5.18, the union's "struggle resolution" (*t'ujaeng kyŏrŭi mun*) de-
clared (among other things) that "Following the examples of the
struggle of our senior comrades, the Kwangju taxi drivers, and the
Taegu taxi laborers' demonstration, numerous vehicle demonstrations, and a general strike, we resolve that we will strive without surrender for the realization of taxi laborers' rights and interests and
human existence." In addition, "we will take the lead in campaigning
for the independence of laborers and the development of this country's democracy as we inherit the fighting spirit of our senior taxi

driver comrades who fought, risking their lives, against the guns and swords of the martial law troops."[17]

Thus the labor movement activists who participated in the event managed to use the 5.18 anniversary as a forum at which they could put forth their own concrete political program (the speeches and proclamations also outlined more specific goals and union demands), successfully evoking the moral power and legitimacy of labor's role in the Kwangju Uprising in support of a larger, contemporary national democratic labor agenda. Far from being pushed to the margins by Kwangju civic leaders, labor movement–sponsored events were part of the official anniversary program. The reason for this, of course, was that the activities of labor were peaceful and low key. Although in previous years representatives from labor groups had carried provocative banners and chanted militant slogans, in 1997 they avoided such displays and consciously distanced themselves from the more radical students.[18] In addition, labor unions brought in participants from outside the Honam area. In 1997, 5.18 leaders were publicly lamenting the fact that although the proclamation of 5.18 as a national commemoration day theoretically made the anniversary a national rather than regional event, in reality it remained a local celebration. How to overcome this problem was a cause for civic concern, and that year, the Democratic Drivers' Day event provided a partial answer.[19] One participant from outside the region confessed that normally he would not want to be anywhere near Kwangju on May 18, but since the Kwangju Uprising was indeed an important historic event in the creation of his union, he had overcome his misgivings to attend.

During the 1980s, *minjung* movement solidarity apparently overrode regional prejudices;[20] in the post-*minjung* 1990s, the dispossessed in Kwangju perhaps face renewed national indifference. While participation in the *minjung* movement may have been a mixed blessing for many different groups during the 1980s, without it, people like the 5.18 victims have much less power.[21] How the interests and demands of 5.18-related and other civic groups in Kwangju will articulate with the programs and strategies of larger national (and international) social movements in the next decades remains to be seen. However, what is clear is that the narratives and practices of commemoration in Kwangju no longer need to stay tied to the discourse(s) of dissent in South Korea. The changing national political context of the 1990s opened a space for competing claims and diverse readings of 5.18 to be articulated in Kwangju itself; with the *minjung* movement weakened, fragmented, and in large part coopted by the state and new middle-class-oriented citizens' movements participating in the institutionalized political sphere, it seems inevitable that the direct victims' groups will be displaced further to the margins.

IN YEARS PAST I HAVE OFTEN HEARD it said in Kwangju that the "5.18 problem" would be "resolved" only when Kim Dae Jung was elected president. Now that the seemingly impossible has come to pass, that notion can be put to the test.

Certainly people in Kwangju feel a very personal connection to Kim Dae Jung. On May 17, 1998, I sat on a folding chair in the vast open plaza of the new cemetery, waiting (with only a few hundred others) for the BFA's annual memorial service to begin. Behind me, I heard a woman explaining to a small child that soon the bereaved family members would be conducting a *chesa* for the 5.18 dead.

"Will the president come?" asked the boy.

"No, he won't," the woman replied.

"Why not?"

"Well, he's too busy. But we know in his heart he wants to be here."

The next morning, May 18, I again sat at the cemetery, witnessing a very different scene but one at which the same kind of optimistic sentiments were expressed. The seats on the plaza were reserved for hundreds of dark-suited dignitaries, so I sat with the crowds of ordinary citizens on the grassy slopes on the sides. Acting Prime Minister Kim Jong-pil would be attending the second annual government-sponsored 5.18 Democratization Movement Commemorative Services, and thousands had come to watch. Thinking of all the years when government officials had been effectively barred from paying respects at the old Mangwŏl-dong cemetery, I asked the middle-aged *ajumŏni* squatting beside me what she thought of Kim Jong-pil's presence there that day.

"Oh, its good," she said, eliciting a chorus of assent from those sitting around us. "What with the economic problems and his upcoming trip to America, the president is too busy to come. Those things are more important than coming here, so he has sent Kim Jong-pil as his representative."

"But . . . it's Kim Jong-pil."[22]

"Oh, that's okay," she answered. "We have achieved democracy, Kim Dae Jung is president—this is right. We are one with the nation now."

Certainly the eighteenth anniversary observances—the first after President Kim took office—were relatively low key, with little political tension; the character of May in 1998 was more in keeping with civic leaders' image of Kwangju as an Asian "Mecca of Democracy" than with *minjung* representations of the site as a symbolic center of antigovernment protest and resistance. Whether the commemoration of 5.18 continues to resemble a civic festival instead of a political demonstration may depend upon whether the high expectations people in the Chŏlla provinces have for Kim Dae Jung's presidency will be realized; it remains to be seen if the wounds of May 1980 will finally be healed. And future discursive treatments of the Kwangju Uprising, different narratives and strategies, and other readings and evocations of its legacy are as yet unimagined.

Notes

5.18 Begins: Violence and Confusion on the City's Streets

1. According to the journalist Tim Shorrock, a cable from the U.S. Defense Intelligence Agency to the Pentagon on May 8, 1980, "noted that Special Forces were trained to use CS gas, a virulent form of tear gas banned in many countries, and had been willing to 'break heads' in previous encounters with Korean students" (Shorrock 1996). People in Kwangju certainly feared them; in May 1980 I heard numerous stories about their ruthlessness and "special training," among them that only orphans were selected for the elite black beret troops. According to a U.S. government statement on Kwangju, U.S. officials in Seoul "reluctantly" agreed to the use of the Twentieth Division to retake Kwangju because that "would be preferable to the continued deployment of the SWC against the citizens of Kwangju" (USIS 1989:16).

As late as 1985 the Korean Ministry of Defense in its official report to the National Assembly on the "incident" was still contending the paratroopers were "young soldiers, carrying out their duty in military turmoil" and that events in Kwangju were a "planned act by impure elements" that threatened the nation's security and survival "both from within and without" (Clark, ed. 1988:83–85). Although there has never been any credible evidence to support the government's contention that 5.18 was a Pyongyang-instigated plot intended to pave the way for a North Korean invasion, the paratroopers were reportedly told they were being sent into Kwangju to suppress a Communist insurrection (*Asian Wall Street Journal*, May 29, 1980, p. A1). The belief that they were fighting Communist insurgents is often cited as an explanation for the paratroopers' brutality (see Eckert et al. 1990:374).

2. See, for example, *Asian Wall Street Journal*, May 16, 1980, p. A1.

3. That is, the partial state of martial law currently in effect was extended to total martial law. Under partial martial law, the civilian government remained in control, but under total martial law, the authority of civilian officials was superceded by that of the military.

4. The so-called "Kim Dae Jung naeran ŭmmo sŏl"—(the theory of Kim Dae Jung's plot of civil turmoil). He was tried, along with twenty-three associates, on charges that included violation of martial law decrees, conspiring to foment revolution, and formation of an antistate organization.

5. "Honam" refers to the geographic area in the extreme southwestern part of the peninsula that includes the southern part of south Ch'ungch'ŏng Province, North and South Chŏlla Provinces, and the island province of Cheju. The southeastern region is known as Yŏngnam.

6. See Cohen and Baker (1991) on the Yusin system and the transition from Park to Chun; also see Clark, ed. (1988:1–14), MacDonald (1996:56–60), and Eckert et al. (1990:359–380).

7. The only property besides government buildings that sustained serious damage was the city's television stations. Citizens angry over biased (and initially nonexistent) domestic news coverage of the uprising targeted the media.

8. Even the journalist Lee Jae-eui, who was inside the Provincial Office Building until May 23, could not escape family pressures. As he poignantly recalls,

After I slept and woke up, I asked a favor of a driver and went to see my mother. That day was my father's *chesa* [death anniversary memorial service], but as soon as I got home I went to bed again. While I was sleeping, all the family members had a meeting.

"It is evident if we leave him alone he will die. We shouldn't leave him in Kwangju. Let's send him to the countryside."

On the morning of the 24th my older brother and sister gave me a bag and said, "Because you have done so much, you need to go to the countryside."

"Today I have an appointment. There are people waiting for me. I have to go."

My older brother dragged me to Sŏbang, without considering my feelings.

I called the Noktu bookstore. I thought, "I want to see my mom and come back, but in this situation if I go home, I won't come back. I am leaving those who will die behind, and running away like a coward."

In the vicinity of Muam-dong I saw citizens carrying coffins and felt agonized, like my heart was breaking, and I felt pain. I looked up the mountain, and the paratroopers were on guard, as if they were waiting for someone (cited in KMHRI 1990:333).

Even on the last night (May 26), families were calling the Provincial Office Building to see if their children were there and begging them to come home. Some young people did leave at the behest of their parents, and in fact the leaders reportedly had students who were at the Provincial Office Building call their families to tell them where they were (Hwang Sŏk Yŏng 1985:234).

9. Until the long distance telephone lines were cut on May 21.

10. See KCS (1997) for personal accounts of journalists who covered the story.

11. That is, they were from the southeastern, or Yŏngnam, region. The Ministry of Defense later claimed that in fact the commander of the Thirty-

third Battalion was a native of Honam, as were 40 percent of the troops sent into Kwangju (Clark, ed. 1988:85).

The "Righteous Rebellion": Citizens Fight Back

1. According to the *New York Times* (May 22, 1980), conservative estimates of the number of demonstrators were fifty to seventy thousand; high estimates suggested as many as two hundred thousand.

2. Opposing forces were hurt as well. For example, four policemen were reportedly run over by a driverless bus in front of the Labor Supervision Office (Hwang Sŏk Yŏng 1985:94).

3. When Lee Jae-eui (in 1980 a junior at Chŏnnam University) wrote *Chugŭmŭl nŏmŏ sidaeŭi ŏtumŭl nŏmŏ* (Beyond death, beyond the darkness of the age) in 1985, he could not publish it under his own name. In fact, the manuscript was written in the utmost secrecy; during most of the 1980s the South Korean government prohibited free discussion of 5.18, and Lee and those who helped him worked in fear that they would be caught by the authorities. When Lee finished the book, he searched for a prominent dissident writer who would be willing to have it published under his name. Not only did Lee and his writing group face arrest if they were known to be the real authors, but the publisher also wanted a "name" to help the book sell. Thus the book originally was printed as the work of the South Chŏlla Social Movement and the famous author Hwang Sŏk Yŏng. Although the police raided the publishing house and seized copies of the text before it could be distributed, it was circulated secretly and became an underground best-seller. In the early 1990s, Lee was revealed as the true author (personal communication from Lee Jae-eui). See also Lee Jae-eui (1999: author's preface).

4. It was still possible to make phone calls within the city.

5. Huntley says this happened May 22, but it is more likely on May 21.

6. Foreign journalists have written about their difficulties getting in and out of the city to report on the Uprising (see KCS 1997). Terry Anderson of the Associated Press recalls his all-night journey on May 21: "We flew to a nearby city, hired a reluctant taxi driver, and headed for Kwangju. At dusk, we were some ten to fifteen kilometers from the city when we began to run into refugees streaming back down the road. They warned us that the road ahead was very dangerous, with small firefights between protestors and soldiers breaking out without warning. The taxi driver stopped the cab and made it clear he intended to go no further. Robin [Moyer] and I got out and began walking down the road" (Anderson 1997:5).

Democracy in Action: The Days of "Free Kwangju"

1. The ability to read Chinese characters is a mark of education in Korea. It would require at least a high school education, and more likely a college degree, to easily understand the flyer. Needless to say, most of the young working-class men involved in the uprising were not college graduates.

2. The full notice is cited in A. Peterson (1995:217–218):

1. The troubles of the 18th past in the Kwangju area have made the maintenance of good order difficult in the extreme; and as regards the behavior by which the harshness of the martial law troops has upset good order in the nation, you are enjoined to maintain an orderliness which will make possible the securing of necessary amends.

2. Viewing the situation now pertaining in the Kwangju area, we know well that the disturbers of the peace who are violating the law and making trouble are not more than a minority, and that the majority of you citizens are upstanding and patriotic Koreans. So that you, and the upstanding citizenry, shall not, within the limits of possibility, suffer wrongful loss on account of the disturbers of the peace who are making the trouble, you are enjoined not to go out into the streets, but to stay strictly inside your houses.

3. Also, so that this distress which means so much to all of you shall not spread further to the disaster of your businesses and your families, it is expected that you will exercise self-control and self-protection and, with an attitude of firm resolve, make it possible to separate out from the disturbers of the peace, thus providing the fullest cooperation with the Martial Law troops for the restoration of good order.

Martial Law Headquarters
Infantry General Lee Hee-seong

3. It now seems certain the *simin'gun* never actually fired from the roof. See Lee Jae-eui (1999:82).

4. For slightly different versions of this public meeting, see A. Peterson (1995:224), who implies there was consensus on turning in the guns; Hwang Sŏk Yŏng (1985:143–146), who suggests there was strong disagreement between the Incident Settlement Committee and ordinary citizens; and Warnberg (1988:42–43), who felt public sentiment was clearly with the insurgents.

5. Wearing of suits by men is a social marker of white-collar (middle-class) status.

6. Other pilgrimage sites include Chŏnnam University, the Kwangju Prison, the Provincial Office Building, Sangmukwan, Kwangju Station, the Mangwŏl-dong cemetery, and Sangmudae, the former army base at the edge of town where prisoners were detained and secret military court trials were held. In 1996 the army base was torn down, and a huge apartment complex was being built in its place. A friend and I, searching for the "5.18 Sacred Sites," walked through the muddy acres of construction area to find, dwarfed by the emerging high-rises, the small cement building that had been used as a courtroom and the barbed-wire-enclosed compound where those held in connection with the uprising had been confined. I was told that only a vigorous civic campaign had saved the buildings and that they would eventually be incorporated into a small park.

7. See Byun and Lewis, eds. (2000) for discussions of the continuing problems of the victims.

8. As stated in the 1985 Ministry of Defense report on the Kwangju incident, Martial Law Command troops "infiltrated agents into Kwangju to locate the deployment of mobsters, and find out the level of their alertness"; their activities included the defusing of explosives in the basement of the Provincial Office Building (Clark, ed. 1988:91). There were many rumors and accusations at the time about progovernment spies. Lee Jae-eui describes his own confrontation with an intelligence officer who had gotten into the "situation room" and the increasing paranoia within the Provincial Office Building about the possible presence of government agents (KMHRI 1990:331; also Hwang Sŏk Yŏng 1985:148–149, 163, 169, 176, and 209–210 for a summary of incidents).

It is widely assumed that agents provocateurs stirred up trouble by planting North Korean spy stories. In one well-known case, the *chojak toen tokch'im sakŏn* (fabricated poison needle incident), a young man, Chang Kye-bŏm, staggered into the Provincial Office Building early in the morning of May 25, yelling that he had been hit with a poison dart. Poison darts were believed to be the special weapons of North Korean spies, and the accusation created turmoil and suspicion among the rebel leadership. Chang was taken to the hospital, but by the time militia members were sent to question him, he had disappeared. Chang was eventually caught and reportedly confessed to passing information to military authorities (Hwang Sŏk Yŏng 1985:183–184). In other cases, those active in the uprising were falsely accused of being North Korean agents. For example, Chŏn Ch'un-sim was a street vendor who had been engaged in street broadcasting; in what she suspects was a government plot, she was identified on two different occasions as a spy and was held and interrogated (KCSPRI 1991:196–198).

9. This is a reference both to the fact that troops traveling through the countryside reportedly took potshots at cows and to the official rationale for the soldiers' actions in firing on civilians—that is, that they were acting in self-defense.

10. To the Student Settlement Committee leaders, who were collecting weapons at the Provincial Office Building with the intention of turning them over to the martial law authorities.

Popular Hopes Die: The Army Retakes the City

1. See Hwang Sŏk Yŏng (1985:231–233) on controversy over numbers.

2. This despite the fact that, according to official U.S. government accounts, Ambassador Gleysteen had concluded that "overreaction by Special Warfare troops was the basic cause of the tragedy" and had urged civilian officials to apologize and to use restraint in retaking the city (USIS 1989:15).

3. Kim was one of those released in the government's Christmas amnesty of 1981.

4. In 1997 Kim Yŏng-ch'ŏl died (personal communication, Byun Juna).

"Kwangju Continues": The Summer of 1980 and Beyond

1. See Cohen and Baker (1991:194–196) for a discussion of the Kim Dae Jung trial and the international response to it.

2. See Communiqué, March 1, 1981, for more information on the trials. Also see Communiqué, October 5, 1980, pp. 7–8 and 11–21, for an account of Kim Dae Jung's difficulty in obtaining legal counsel and his trial.

3. Allegations of torture were common throughout the Park, Chun, and even Roh Tae Woo eras. See Cohen and Baker (1991:198–200).

4. It appears the taking of family members as hostages was not uncommon. I was stunned when interviewing a prominent 5.18 activist, a minister, in 1996 to hear him calmly relate how he was hiding with Canadian missionaries in the summer of 1980, but when the police kidnapped his young son, he was forced to turn himself in.

5. See Clark (1991) for a general analysis of anti-Americanism in South Korea. Also see Part III for more extensive discussion of Kwangju and anti-Americanism.

6. From materials presented at the second annual 5.18 Kwangju People's Uprising Injured Persons' Association seminar held in Kwangju, May 24, 1997.

Truth Telling in the Fifth Republic

1. See author's preface to the English translation (Lee Jae-eui 1999).

2. For example, officers of the Youth Federation for the Promotion of Democratization were jailed for producing and distributing leaflets on 5.18 "slandering" the government in May 1985 (see *Seoul shinmun,* May 10, 1985, and *Tonga ilbo,* May 13, 1985); police in Kwangju seized three thousand copies of a volume entitled "National Realities and the Regional Movement" in December 1985 (*Choson ilbo,* December 14, 1985); and "antigovernment" printed matter, a VCR, and three videos on 5.18 were confiscated at a church in Kyonggi-do in October 1986 (*Choson ilbo,* October 25, 1986).

3. See International League for Human Rights (1985:ch. 4) for a detailed discussion of press restrictions in the Fifth Republic.

4. See Clark, ed. (1988:83–92) for full document.

5. See MacDonald (1996:123) on the end of the Chun era.

6. Refers to the conviction of Kim Dae Jung in connection with 5.18. See Part I.

7. Originally presented as a paper on a panel about the Kwangju Uprising at the April 1987 annual meetings of the Association for Asia Studies and subsequently published in Clark, ed. 1988.

8. See Part I, pp. 40–41 for a fuller explanation of "participation." Also p. 48 for example of giving money.

9. See Han (1980) for an excellent analysis of the historical role of students in political protest.

10. See Part I, p. 38.

11. See Part I, pp. 4, 12 on student participation.

12. The government insisted the allegations were the "groundless rumors" that "impure elements" fabricated to inflame the local populace, instigate the rioting, and prolong the whole episode.

13. See Part I, p. 18 on response to American inaction.

14. The film is based on a short story, "There a Petal Silently Falls," by novelist Choi Yun.

15. According to director Jang Sun-woo, it is "a movie that reveals how human beings disintegrated under violence" and explores the correlation between the brutality of political and sexual violence. "Quite distorted would have been a portrait of the year 1980 because of the tremendous political violence. Instead of tackling the subject head on, I chose to make a detour to disclose the brutality of political violence through the ordeals of an innocent girl who falls prey to sexual exploitation" (cited in Koh 1996:W2).

16. Initially the prosecution concluded the firing by martial law troops was "accidental," as soldiers tried to protect themselves (see *Korea Herald,* November 26, 1995, p. 3). The prosecution reversed itself on this point after the enactment of the special law.

17. See Clark, ed. (1988:93–94) for a statement from the U.S. side on the issue of operational control.

18. See M. Peterson (1988) for the U.S. side of the story as told by the officials (Ambassador Gleysteen and General Wickham) who were involved at the time.

19. Sponsored by the Washington-based Center for Development Policy, the demonstrating groups included the following: the United Movement for Democracy and Reunification in Korea, the Commission on the Kwangju Massacre, the Commission on U.S.-Asian Relations, the North American Coalition for Human Rights in Korea, the Council for Democracy in Korea (New York), and the Korean Committee for Democracy in Korea (Philadelphia).

20. It was the mid-1990s before a major Seoul department store opened a branch in Kwangju, although the downtown had acquired more stylish shops.

21. As cited in Cho (1989).

22. See Lee Chae-jin (1971:106–117).

Kwangju in the 1990s

1. Refrain from "May," a popular 5.18 song.

2. From "The Song of Going to the Kwangju Battle," a popular 5.18 song.

3. From the Commemoration Events Program of the Commemoration Events Committee. This number compares with thirty-six events in 1997 and forty-four in 1996.

4. About twenty thousand people reportedly attended the event in 1998 (*Chŏnnam ilbo,* May 18, 1998, p. 14).

5. See Choi Chungmoo (1995, 1997) for history and analysis of *madangguk* and its place in the *minjung* culture movement; also see Kim Kwang-ok (1994:208–209). *"Minjung"* refers literally to "masses" or "people"; it is, as Abelmann says, "a noun and adjective that could in the 1980s be combined with almost anything—history, music, art, film, religion, economics, etc." (1997:251). Koo defines the concept of *minjung* as "an ideology and a political strategy" and the "dominant antihegemonic ideology" after the Kwangju Uprising; the Korean *minjung* movement of the 1970s and 1980s was a "class-based political movement" (1993a:144, 145). *Minjung* is "a broad ideology, touching on economic, political, and social realities in society. Economically, it rejects depen-

dent capitalist development and advocates a radical restructuring of the economy in order to achieve distributive justice; politically, it elevates national unification to the position of ultimate goal, and to this end it seeks to repel the anticommunist security ideology and to end U.S. intervention in Korean affairs; socially and culturally, it promotes concepts of national identity and independence. And as a political strategy *minjung* activists seek to forge a close alliance among students, industrial workers, and small farmers" (Koo 1993a:144). For other discussions, see the essays in Wells, ed. (1995b), Abelmann (1993).

6. See King (1983:43–45) for a brief description of traditional mask dance theater; also see Choi Chungmoo for the contemporary version's function as an "open forum anticipating audience participation and communication" (1995:115).

7. See Kim Kwang-ok (1994) for an excellent discussion of the use of folk culture, particularly shamanic rituals, as a language of resistance in the 1980s.

8. In a traditional Korean house, the *madang* is the open courtyard or yard; in a farming community, it also was the term used for an open space where communal activities such as threshing were carried out and mask-dance dramas and shamanistic ritual festivals were performed. See Choi Chungmoo (1995: 114–115) for a discussion of its meaning in the development of *madangguk*.

9. Characters in *madangguk* typically speak in Chŏlla dialect (Choi Chungmoo 1997:367).

10. *Pansori* is a traditional, narrative folk vocal art form performed by one singer.

11. White hemp is the color and fabric from which mourning clothes traditionally are made. Today female members of the bereaved families distinguish themselves at memorial rites by wearing white *hanbok*, although the men wear black suits.

12. See charts in KMHRI (1990:1545–1553), which include demographic information on victims.

13. That is, *minjung* as political historical actors, a position that "exalts *minjung* political activity and draws on this legacy for continued revolutionary activity" (Abelmann 1993:139–140). Further, "in the dialectic between *minjung* subjectivity and national subjectivity, *minjung* are realized as subjects in national struggle" (Abelmann 1993:142). Also see Abelmann (1993) for a discussion of the distinction between *minjung* as subject and *minjung* as cultural practice.

14. By the 1990s *minjung* activism had all but disappeared from public view—Abelmann in fact refers to "post*minjung* South Korea" (1997:253)— although there is speculation and disagreement about the future of the movement. Some focus on the development of civil society in a newly democratic Korea (see Kim Sunhyuk 1996) or, more broadly, state–society relations in Korea (see Koo 1993b). Others suggest that democratization opened a space for political participation by the middle class, which then deserted the *minjung* movement. Remnants of the *minjung* movement continue, however, in movements such as labor and in the more moderate agendas of other social groups (see Choi Jang Jip 1996).

15. May 18 was designated as a nationally observed commemoration day in 1997.

16. Cited in *Korea Times,* May 19, 1998, p. 2.

17. *Newsweek* international edition; see also the cover of the *Time* international edition, June 2, 1980, and photos in Hwang and Kim (1991:esp. 56, 64, 87, 88, and 90.

The Construction of Memory and the 5.18 Movement: An Overview

1. The Roh era began with the election of December 1987, in which only 4.8 percent of the voters in Kwangju supported the ruling party (Cumings 1997:389).

2. See Abelmann (1997) on the farmers' movement in the 1990s, Thomas (1993) on squatters, and Kim Seung-kyung (1997) on women and the labor movement.

Making Martyrs and Patriotic Heroes: Direct Victims' Groups and the Legitimation of 5.18

1. The Kwangju telephone directory in 1996 listed at least thirteen 5.18–related groups. Over the years various coalition groups have come and gone, as have some associations (occasionally nationwide) formed for specific campaigns (for example, the prosecution movement of the late 1980s).

2. See, for example, BFA (1989:339–343) for a discussion of the complications of qualifying as an official "injured person" and pp. 331–332 for a list of the dead whose families (as of 1989) had not received compensation because the victims were classified as "mobsters" or "rioters" (*p'okto/nandongja*); see also KCSPRI (1991:242–243) for a discussion of categories of victims.

3. See BFA (1989:312, 323) for an accounting of the missing as of April 1991 and a listing of victims whose identity and/or circumstances of death remain unconfirmed.

4. Ideological differences have been particularly divisive among groups of those who were arrested/detained. Some 5.18 activists feel the government encouraged groups to split in the mid-1980s as a deliberate attempt to weaken the 5.18 movement; others attribute the fragmentation of the movement to the pursuit of self-interest on the part of the direct victims.

5. The NSL is part of the anti-Communist legacy of the post–World War II period of American occupation of Korea. Passed on December 1, 1948, it branded as criminals those who "in collusion with a betrayer sought to consolidate or group together with the object of disturbing the tranquility of the state" (cited in Henderson 1991:150). Its vague wording gives the authorities broad powers to arrest and imprison anyone accused of forming an antistate organization—interpreted during the 1970s and 1980s as meaning any group critical of the government or whose activities the authorities did not like or found threatening. Frequent abuse of the NSL by the government has led to popular calls for its repeal and/or reform; President Kim Dae Jung promised to change the NSL but (as of 1999) had not yet done so. See Henderson (1991)

for the history of the NSL; also see Yoon (1990:171–177) for constitutional issues and the NSL.

6. Personal communication from members of the Kwangju chapter of Min'gahyŏp.

7. Not all 5.18 victims were originally buried in Mangwŏl-dong. Traditionally, Koreans are buried in auspiciously located family plots near their ancestral (lineage) homes. See Yujokhoe (1989), which gives the location of the grave of each victim; many appear to be in rural villages. In 1980, the Kwangju Municipal Cemetery (within which is the Mangwŏl-dong Cemetery with the 5.18 plots) was not a particularly desirable place to be buried; that it was the final resting place for so many victims from the beginning is suggestive of the socioeconomic status of their families. By the mid-1990s Korean burial practices were being thought of as a social problem. According to the Health and Welfare Ministry, in 1995 graveyards occupied fully 1 percent of the nation's land, and 69 percent were in the form of individual mounds; this practice (and the avoidance of public cemeteries) was said to be destructive of the natural environment and barred effective land use (*Korea Times*, April 6, 1995). By the late 1990s it was not unusual for a visitor to witness a funeral at Mangwŏl-dong, and the vast public space around the 5.18 corner was filling up.

8. In a speech on May 18, 1995, ruling party chairman Roh Tae Woo said the following of 5.18: "It was not only regrettable that social confusion followed the October 26 incident, but also it was a national tragedy that in the vortex of the confusion as many as 191 human lives were lost." This was the first public mention of its kind by a government and ruling party leader (*Tonga ilbo* editorial, May 20, 1985).

9. Personal communication from Sherrill Davis.

10. See Kwang-kyu Lee (1987:66–69), Janelli and Janelli (1982:90–92), and Deuchler (1987) for general discussions of ancestor rituals in Korean society and descriptions of the conduct of ancestral rites.

11. After the move to the new cemetery in 1997 this communal banquet continued to be held but in the History Gate Pavilion rest area to the side of the central plaza rather than around the graves themselves.

12. Compare with Kwang-kyu Lee (1989:175–177) on contemporary urban practice.

13. The popular culture movement vocabulary was commonly employed in other parts of the Uprising anniversary program into the late 1990s. The Uprising Eve parade in the mid-1990s, for example, included shamanic imagery and funereal elements. See also Kendall (1996:71–82) for a discussion of the political meanings to be found in the revival of traditional Confucian-style wedding rituals during the 1980s.

14. See Janelli and Janelli (1982:ch. 5) for a discussion of the functions of lineage ancestral rites.

15. When some compensation was given to the families of the dead immediately after the Uprising, for example, the relatives of thirty-six of the dead classified by the government as mobsters or rioters did not receive any money. See Pak Wonsoon (1995:30).

16. It is worth noting here that the first title for the bereaved families' group, the 5.18 Kwangju Righteous Uprising Bereaved Families' Association

(BFA 1989: 357), is a name that evokes such historic actions as the "Righteous Army" of elite and peasant guerrilla bands that "manifested the will of the Korean people to oppose Japan" through armed resistance at the turn of the century (Chung 1995:68).

17. The April 3,1948, uprising on the island of Cheju was actually a series of attacks on police stations by pro-Communist guerrillas who opposed the upcoming elections. It began a cycle of violence and repression on the island that resulted in as many as thirty thousand deaths. See Merrill (1980) for one of the few English-language accounts.

18. In some cases their parents disapproved. One young man confessed he felt uncomfortable standing beside me because as a foreigner, I was a magnet for journalists. He feared his picture would end up on the evening news and thus his father would discover he had gone to Kwangju.

19. I heard both of these stories from MPA members with whom I visited the sites in 1996. We were accompanying an American archaeologist who was there to give an estimate of what it might cost, in time and money, to excavate the areas.

20. Personal communication from Seventeenth Anniversary Events Committee official.

21. As of May 1997, as cited by the chairman of the association at the second annual 5.18 Injured People's Association scholarly meeting.

22. 1994 Kwangju City government statistics break down the official victims into 154 dead, 47 official missing, 2,710 injured, and 505 questioned/detained/convicted. Other groups calculate that the number is higher—for example, that there are 107 "unofficial" missing—and the Injured People's Association claims higher numbers of injured (as cited in Byun 1997). In addition, there are the 120 wounded who have died since 1980. These statistics do not include victims' families (the "indirect victims"), who are also recognized as being at increased risk. The rate of death may also be increasing; in one eight-month period in 1994–1995, nine of the injured died (cited by Byun 1997), and in 1998 two famous victims finally succumbed (personal communication from Byun Juna).

23. Causation as explained by the survivors' families (personal communication from Byun Juna); see also Lee Jae-eui (1995:101) for examples. *Hwabyŏng* is a Korean culture-bound syndrome in which death is attributed to excessive *hwa*, or pent-up anger, frustration, and resentment. See Lin (1983).

24. Personal communication from IPA chairman.

25. Only when Dr. Byun Juna, a medical anthropologist and nurse, began working with them in the mid-1990s did this problem come to light (personal communication from IPA chairman).

26. Personal communication, 1996.

27. In 2000 a committee to establish a 5.18 memorial human rights clinic was formed (personal communication from Byun Juna).

28. See Byun and Lewis, eds. (2000) for discussions of the connection between the victims' health and human rights.

29. The AD is relatively recently established. There have been a succession of groups comprised of those who were arrested, including a number of 5.18 umbrella/coalition groups led by prominent detainees. The AD group was

formed in 1997 to fill a gap. I was told that the AD has about one thousand members (personal communication from AD chairman, 1998).

30. Personal communication, 1996.

31. Popular enough to be a candidate for "official 5.18 song" in 1997 (personal communication from Lee Jae-eui).

32. See above for an account of the journalist Bradley Martin's meeting with Yun.

The Uprising as Civic Asset:
New Citizens' Groups and the Reimaging of Kwangju

1. One tour map of Kwangju, with a nod perhaps to the annual October Kimchee Festival, added a third attraction and referenced Kwangju as "a City of Arts, Justice, and Flavor."

2. The chairman was a direct victim as well. He had participated as a member of the Incident Settlement Committee in 1980 (see KMHRI 1990:186–196).

3. The situation changed with the election of Kim Dae Jung in 1997; by 2000, the foundation was able to distribute grants for such 5.18–related projects as a scholarly conference in Los Angeles, jointly hosted by USC and UCLA.

4. Over two hundred nongovernmental organizations directly participated in the drafting process of the charter that began in 1994. The final drafting meeting took place in Hong Kong in 1996, and its public declaration in 1998 coincided with the fiftieth anniversary of the Universal Declaration on Human Rights. See KCS (1998).

5. *Mudŭng ilbo,* a local newspaper, along with the Journalists' Association of Korea, cosponsored the event.

6. Personal communication from KCS Executive Committee member.

7. *P'yong* is a Korean unit of area equivalent to about six square feet.

What Is the "Kwangju Spirit"?

1. Prostitutes did reportedly participate; see Hwang Sŏk Yŏng (1985:117–118) for the blood donation incident; also see KCSPRI (1991:118).

2. See Choi Jang Jip (1993) and Eckert (1993) for discussions of the middle class and the 1987 democratic transformation.

3. See Lee Samsung (1988) for an extensive analysis of Kwangju and anti-Americanism in Korea; also see Clark's seminal article (1991) for a different perspective on the same issue.

4. According to *Chosŏn ilbo,* February 1, 1989, the ACC in Kwangju was attacked and/or seized twice in 1981, three times in 1982, four times in 1983, twice in 1984, twice in 1985, once in 1986, three times in 1987, and eight times in 1988.

5. The original plan apparently was to reopen in April 1990 (just before the tenth anniversary of 5.18)— an idea condemned as foolhardy by Korean

authorities (*Tonga ilbo,* April 13, 1990). Many in 5.18 circles opposed the reopening (one leader reportedly said the ACC had closed in the face of citizens' struggles against unconvincing U.S. attitudes about the Uprising and called reopening it an "impetuous action disregarding realities"), but at least one prominent figure not only argued in favor of the center's importance, but also helped the U.S. ambassador cut the ribbon at the new building (*Hank'gyŏre sinmun,* June 9, 1990).

Remembering Kwangju in Post-*Minjung* Korea

1. "Blue dreams" mean idealism.
2. Taedong flowers grow along the banks of the Taedong River in North Korea; the reference here is to reunification.
3. Cited in *Chŏnnam ilbo,* May 19, 1997; p. 20.
4. See Kim Sankyu (2000) for a discussion of the treatment of the disabled in Korea and the relationship of this issue to the 5.18 victims.
5. It is hard to know exactly when this term came into common parlance, but certainly by the mid-1980s it was being used in Kwangju. For the first few years even activist groups in Kwangju referred to it as the "Kwangju Incident," then for a time 5.18 groups used "Kwangju Righteous Uprising" (Kwangju Ŭigŏ).
6. During the eighteenth anniversary, for example, semipermanent signs in the new cemetery that carried the "Democratization Movement" designation were simply covered over with banners using the "People's Uprising" title when Kwangju groups used the space for their particular events. According to one civic leader, there is no problem using either name; scholars and those in Kwangju simply prefer the "People's Uprising" because it is more accurate and "more meaningful." However, in my experience, referring to it as the "5.18 People's Uprising" in lectures and discussions outside of the Honam region made Korean academics uncomfortable, and I was told more than once that calling it that was clearly a political statement.
7. Observation of lawyer Kim Dae-bong; cited in the *Chŏnnam ilbo,* May 19, 1997, p. 20.
8. Indeed, one of the explicit governing principles for screening events in 1997 was that they be nonpolitical and noncommercial in nature (AEC 1997b:2).
9. But perhaps no other members of the audience were afflicted with visions of Kwangju citizens being chased through the forest.
10. Previous to this, Hanch'ongnyŏn (National Federation of Student Councils), a radical student governing association, had planned to hold its inaugural meeting in Kwangju. Local newspapers heard about the plan and reported it; public opinion was sufficiently aroused that Hanch'ongnyŏn was forced to change the proposed venue (personal communication from Lee Jae-eui). For more on Hanch'ongnyŏn, see below.
11. As many as five thousand radical students held street demonstrations on May 23. See, for example, Kim Hŭng-gi and Ku Kil-yong in *Kwangnam ilbo,* May 24, 1997, p. 23.
12. Initiated in 1993, in 1996 Hanch'ongnyŏn was an umbrella organiza-

tion representing student councils of some 180 universities and colleges in Korea and was characterized by increasingly violent tactics and a radical platform. In August 1996 Hanch'ongnyŏn was responsible for nine days of violent demonstrations at Yonsei University, during which a building was seized.

13. Even students in Kwangju apparently felt the same way. A survey taken at Chŏnnam University in the aftermath of the Yonsei University incident found that 63.9 percent of the students and 50 percent of the faculty found Hanch'ongnyŏn's cause acceptable but its methods wrong (*Korea Times*, September 7, 1996, p. 1).

14. See Ogle (1990) on the history of the Korean labor movement through the 1980s; also see Koo (1993a) on the relationship between the *minjung* movement and the labor movement. As Ogle states, "The Kwangju massacre was the calamity that laid Korea's authoritarianism open on the table for all to see, and it has become the analogy through which much of labor's sufferings have been interpreted" (1990:161).

15. Officially the event is called the "5.18 Democratic Drivers' Day Memorial Service and Rally for Laborers' Determination to Keep the Spirit Alive" (5.18 Minjukisa ŭi Nal mit Chŏngsin'gyesŭng ŭl wihan Nodongja Kyŏlŭi Taehŭi).

16. As reported in the *Mudŭng ilbo*, May 21, 1997, p. 1.

17. From "Chŏn'guk minju t'aeksi nodongchohapyŏngmaeng t'ujaeng kyŏlŭi mun" (National democratic taxi labor union struggle resolution), statement read at the Provincial Office Building, Kwangju, May 20, 1997.

18. Reportedly, taxi drivers from out of town rode in buses in the parade rather than walking (as had been planned) so that students could not infiltrate their ranks and cause a disturbance when they reached the Provincial Office Building (personal communication from union official from Taegu).

19. See panel discussion among 5.18 civic leaders reported in *Chŏnnam ilbo*, May 19, 1997, p. 20.

20. Albeit incompletely. Choi Chungmoo points out that in the *minjung* "discursive space of resistance . . . the people of Chŏlla Province now have become allegorical icons" (1997:367). On the other hand, Choi Jang Jip (1993:44), for example, points out that the vertical division of society along regional lines, in the form of discrimination against the Chŏlla provinces, is one reason the ruling elites were able to remain in power in 1987. Further, regionalism in Korea represents not some "irrational, collective sentiment or ideology," but rather is the "cumulative result of other conflictual factors like political and economic democratization whose failure has strengthened discrimination against a particular region" (p. 45).

21. Cf. Thomas' study of the squatters' movement, in which he says that "although this [*minjung*] movement was the only national political force that acted on behalf of and provided consistent support to disadvantaged and disempowered groups, it never focused exclusively on the interests of those groups" (1993:235). For the interrelationship between the *minjung* movement and other social movements see also Kim Seung-kyung (1997) and Abelmann (1996).

22. It was then Lieutenant Colonel Kim Jong-pil who helped his uncle-by-marriage Park Chung Hee seize control of the government in 1961 in a coup

that placed the military at the center of Korean politics, where it would re-main for the next three decades. Kim Jong-pil was also the architect (and first head) of the dreaded Korean Central Intelligence Agency. Ousted from power by Park in the mid-1970s, Kim Jong-pil went on to find rehabilitation as an opposition politician—one of the "three Kims" of the 1980s. See Eckert et al. (1990:359–372).

Bibliography

Abelmann, Nancy. 1993. "*Minjung* Theory and Practice." In *Cultural National-ism in East Asia: Representation and Identity*, ed. Harumi Befu. Berkeley: In-stitute of East Asian Studies. Research Papers and Policy Studies.

———. 1996. *Echoes of the Past, Epics of Dissent: A South Korean Social Move-ment*. Berkeley: University of California Press.

———. 1997. "Reorganizing and Recapturing Dissent in 1990s South Korea." In *Between Resistance and Revolution*, ed. Richard Fox and Orin Starn. New Brunswick, N.J.: Rutgers University Press.

AD (Association of the Detained) (5.18 Kwangju Minjung Hangjaeng Kusok-chahoe). 1997. *Hamkke hanŭn owŏl* [May,together]. Kwangju:Hansol Pub-lishers.

AEC (Anniversary Events Committee). 1995. *5.18 sŏngji sullye* [5.18 sacred places pilgrimage tour].

———. 1997a. *5.18 Minjung Hangjaeng 17 chunyŏn charyojip* [5.18 People's Up-rising 17th anniversary information pamphlet].

———. 1997b. "5.18 Minjung Hangjaeng che 17 kinyŏmhaengsa sogae" [In-troduction to the 5.18 People's Uprising 17th anniversary events]. Un-published document.

Anderson, Terry. 1997. "Remembering Kwangju." In KCS 1997.

BFA (Bereaved Families' Association) (5.18 Kwangju Minjung Hangjaeng Yujokhoe). 1989. *Kwangju Minjung Hangjaeng Pimangnok* [Kwangju People's Uprising memorial book]. Seoul: Tosŏ Publishers.

Brandt, Vincent S.R. 1971. *A Korean Village: Between Farm and Sea*. Cambridge: Harvard University Press.

Byun Juna. 1996. "Fifteen-Year Aftermath Syndrome of Victims from the Kwang-ju Civil Uprising of May 18, 1980, South Korea." Unpublished paper.

———. 1997. "5.18 Minjuhwa Undong p'ihaejadŭlŭi changaehyŏn hwang kwa daech'aek" [5.18 democratization movement victims' current obsta-cles and countermeasures]. Lecture presented at 2d annual 5.18 Injured People's Association scholarly meeting, Kwangju, May 24, 1997.

————. 2000. "The 15 Year Aftermath Trauma." In Byun and Lewis, eds.

Byun Juna, and Linda S. Lewis, eds. 2000. *The 1980 Kwangju Uprising after 20 Years: The Unhealed Wounds of the Victims*. Seoul: Dahae Publishing Company.

Catholic Church, Kwangju Diocese Peace and Justice Committee (Ch'ŏnju-kyo Kwangju Daekyogu Chŏngŭi P'yŏnghwa Wiwŏnhoe). 1988. *Kwangju simin sahoe ŭisik chosa* [A study of Kwangju citizens' social consciousness through popular feelings about the Kwangju Uprising]. Kwangju: Pit'koŭl Publishing. Cited as PJC.

Cho Choong-Bin. 1989. "Regionalism in Korea: A Search for a Synthetic View." Unpublished conference paper.

Choi Chungmoo. 1995. "The Minjung Culture Movement and Popular Culture." In Wells, ed.

————. 1997. "The Discourse of Decolonization and Popular Memory: South Korea." In *Formations of Colonial Modernity in East Asia,* ed. Tani E. Barlow. Durham: Duke University Press.

Choi Jang Jip. 1993. "Political Cleavages in South Korea." In Koo, ed.

————. 1996. "Social Movements and Class in South Korea." Paper presented at the Association for Asian Studies annual meeting.

Chung Chai-sik. 1995. "Confucian Tradition and Nationalist Ideology in Korea." In Wells, ed.

Clark, Donald N. 1991. "Bitter Friendship: Understanding Anti-Americanism in South Korea." In *Korea Briefing, 1991,* ed. Donald N. Clark. Boulder: Westview Press.

————, ed. 1988. *The Kwangju Uprising: Shadows over the Regime in South Korea.* Boulder: Westview Press.

Cohen, Jerome, and Edward J. Baker. 1991. "U.S. Foreign Policy and Human Rights in South Korea." In William Shaw, ed.

Communiqué. *See* Japan Emergency Christian Conference on Korean Problems.

CSPRI (Chŏnnam Social Problems Research Institute) (Chŏnnam Sahoe Munjae Yŏn'guso). 1988. *5.18 Kwangju Minjung Hangjaeng charyojip* [5.18 Kwangju People's Uprising collected documents]. Kwangju: Dosŏch'ulp'an.

Cumings, Bruce. 1984. "The Historical Significance of the Kwangju Rebellion." Unpublished paper.

————. 1997. *Korea's Place in the Sun.* New York: W.W. Norton.

————. 1999. "Introduction." In Lee Jai-eui.

Deuchler, Martina. 1987. " Neo-Confucianism in Action: Agnation and Ancestor Worship in Early Yi Korea." In Kendall and Dix, eds.

Eckert, Carter. 1993. "The South Korean Bourgeoisie: A Class in Search of Hegemony." In Koo, ed.

———— et al. 1990. *Korea Old and New: A History.* Cambridge, Mass.: Korea Institute, Harvard University. Seoul: Ilchokak Publishers.

Foard, James H. 1994. "The Universal and the Particular in the Rites of Hiroshima." In Keyes, Kendall, and Hardacre, eds.

Han Sunjoo. 1980. "Student Activism: A Comparison between the 1960 Uprising and the 1971 Protest Movement." In *Political Participation in Korea,* ed. Chung Lim Kim. Santa Barbara: Clio Books.

Henderson, Gregory. 1991. "Human Rights in South Korea, 1945–1953." In Shaw, ed.

Huntley, Martha. 1982. "Should We Tell You about This?" *Presbyterian Survey,* March 1982.

Hwang Chong Kŏn and Kim Nyŏng Man. 1991. *Kwangju, kŭnal* [Kwangju, that day]. Seoul: Sajinyesulsa.

Hwang Sŏk Yŏng. 1985. *Chugŭmŭl nŏmŏ sidaeŭi ŏdumŭl nŏmŏ: Kwangju 5 wŏl Minjung Hangjaengŭi kirok* [Beyond death, beyond the darkness of the age: A record of the Kwangju May People's Uprising]. Seoul: P'ulpit.

ICNDK (International Christian Network for Democracy in Korea). 1990. *Minju dongji* 68, 69 (June, July).

International League for Human Rights and the International Human Rights Law Group. 1985. *Democracy in South Korea: A Promise Unfulfilled.* New York: International League for Human Rights.

Janelli, Roger L., and Dawnhee Yim Janelli. 1982. *Ancestor Worship and Korean Society.* Stanford: Stanford University Press.

Japan Emergency Christian Conference on Korean Problems. October 5, 1980. *Korea Communiqué* 37.

———. March 1, 1981. *Korea Communiqué* 38.

———. May 10, 1981. *Korea Communiqué* 39.

———. July 4, 1981. *Korea Communiqué* 40. Cited as Communiqué.

Kang, K. Connie. 1996. "Three South Koreans Find Aid in L.A. for '80 Wounds." *Los Angeles Times,* February 5, p. B1.

KCS (Kwangju Citizens' Solidarity). 1995. "Kwangju: Mecca of Democracy." Unpublished pamphlet.

———. 1996a. "Introduction: Kwangju Citizens' Solidarity." Http://www.ik.co.kr/kcs.

———. 1996b. "Proceedings of the First International Youth Camp for Human Rights and Peace." Unpublished conference papers.

———. 1997. *Kwangju in the Eyes of the World: The Personal Recollections of the Foreign Correspondents Covering the Kwangju Uprising.* Kwangju: Pulpit Publishing.

———. 1998. "Program: Declaring the Asian Human Rights Charter." Http://www.ik.co.kr/kcs.

KCSPRI (Korean Christian Social Problems Research Institute) (Han'guk Kidokkyo Sahoe Munje Yŏn'guwon). 1991. *Kwangju Minjung Hangjaeng kwa yŏsŏng* [The Kwangju People's Uprising and Women]. Seoul: Minjungsa.

Kendall, Laurel. 1985. *Shamans, Housewives, and Other Restless Spirits: Women in Korean Ritual Life.* Honolulu: University of Hawai'i Press.

———. 1996. *Getting Married in Korea: Of Gender, Morality, and Modernity.* Berkeley: University of California Press.

Kendall, Laurel, and Griffin Dix, eds. 1987. *Religion and Ritual in Korean Society.* Berkeley: Center for Korean Studies, University of California. Korea Research Monograph 12.

Keyes, Charles F., Laurel Kendall, and Helen Hardacre, eds. 1994. *Asian Visions of Authority.* Honolulu: University of Hawai'i Press.

Kim Kwang-ok. 1994. "Rituals of Resistance: The Manipulation of Shamanism in Contemporary Korea." In Keyes, Kendall, and Hardacre, eds.

————. 1996. "The Reproduction of Confucian Culture in Contemporary Korea." In *Confucian Traditions and East Asian Modernity*, ed. Tu Wei-ming. Cambridge, Mass.: Harvard University Press.

Kim Sangkyu. 2000. "The Government's Responsibility and Role in the Victims' Rehabilitation." In Byun and Lewis, eds.

Kim Seong Nae. 1989. "Lamentations of the Dead: The Historical Imagery of Violence on Cheju Island, South Korea." *Journal of Ritual Studies* 3, 2 (Summer):251–285.

Kim Seung-kyung. 1997. *Class Struggle or Family Struggle? The Lives of Women Factory Workers in South Korea*. London: Cambridge University Press.

Kim Sŏng-su. 1997. "5.18 pusanghu samangja silt'ae" [Conditions of Those Who Died after Being Injured in 5.18]. Unpublished paper presented at the second annual 5.18 Injured People's Association scholarly meeting, Kwangju, May 24, 1997.

Kim Sunhyuk. 1996. "Civil Society in South Korea: From Grand Democracy Movements to Petty Interest Groups?" *Journal of Northeast Asian Studies*, Summer.

King, Eleanor. 1983. "Reflections on Korean Dance." In Korean National Commission for UNESCO, *Korean Dance, Theatre, and Cinema*. Seoul: Sisa-yong-o-sa Publishers.

KMHRI (Korean Modern Historical Materials Research Institute) (Han'guk Hyŏndaesa Saryo Yŏnguso—Hyŏnsayŏn). 1990. *Kwangju Ohwŏl Mingjung Hangjaeng Saryo chŏnjip* [The Complete Collection of the Historical Record of the Kwangju May People's Uprising]. Seoul: P'ulpit.

Koh Chik-mann. 1996. "Jang's Poetic, Magical Realism Flourishes in 'A Petal.'" *Korean Times*, March 22, p. W-2.

Koo, Hagen. 1993a. "The State, *Minjung*, and the Working Class in South Korea." In Koo, ed.

————. 1993b. "Strong State and Contentious Society." In Koo, ed.

————, ed. 1993. *State and Society in Contemporary Korea*. Ithaca: Cornell University Press.

Kwangju City. 1997. *5.18 Yujokchi annae* [Information about the glorious achievements of 5.18].

Kwangju City, May 18 History Compilation Committee (Kwangju 5.18 Saryo P'yŏnch'an Wiwŏnhoe). 1997. *5.18 Kwangju Minjung Hangjaeng* [The 5.18 Kwangju Peoples' Uprising]. Kwangju: Tosŏ Publishing.

————. 1998. *The May 18 Kwangju Democratic Uprising*. Trans. Lee Kyung-soon and Ellen Bishop. Kwangju: Kwangju City Government.

Lee Chae-jin. 1971. "Urban Political Competition in a Developing Nation." *Comparative Political Studies*, April, p. 106–116.

Lee Jae-eui. 1995. "Kwangju's Democratic Citizens Bemoan Successful Coup d'Etat" [Sŏnggonghan 'k'udet'ae sinŭm' hanŭn Kwangju minju simin] *Modern Praxis* 14.

————. 1999. *Kwangju Diary: Beyond Death, Beyond the Darkness of the Age*. Trans. by Kap Su Seol and Nick Mamatas. UCLA Asian Pacific Monograph Series. Los Angeles: University of California. (Originally published in Korean, with Hwang Sŏk Yŏng as author.)

Lee Kwang-Kyu. 1987. "Ancestor Worship and Kinship Structure in Korea." In Kendall and Dix, eds.

———. 1989. "The Practice of Traditional Family Rituals in Contemporary Urban Korea." *Journal of Ritual Studies* 3, 2 (Summer):167–183.

Lee, Samsung. 1988. "Kwangju and America in Perspective." *Asian Perspective* 12, 2 (Fall–Winter):69–122.

Lewis, Linda. 1988a. "The 'Kwangju Incident' Observed: An Anthropological Perspective on Civil Uprisings." In Clark, ed.

———. 1988b. "City of Light/City of Outlaws: Kwangju and the Construction of an Urban Identity." Paper presented at American Anthropological Association annual meeting, November.

Lin, K. M. 1983. "Hwa-Byung: A Korean Culture-Bound Syndrome?" *American Journal of Psychiatry* 140, 1 (January):105–107.

Macdonald, Donald S. 1996. *The Koreans: Contemporary Politics and Society*, 3d ed. Boulder: Westview Press.

Martin, Bradley. 1997. "Yun Sang Won: The Knowledge in Those Eyes." In KCS 1997.

Merrill, John. 1980. "The Cheju-do Rebellion." *Journal of Korean Studies* 2: 177.

NACHRK (North American Coalition for Human Rights in Korea). 1980. *Reports from Kwangju*. Washington, D.C.

Ogle, George. 1990. *South Korea: Dissent within the Economic Miracle*. London: Zed Books.

Pak Wonsoon. 1995. "Kwangjunŭn kyesok toego itta" [Kwangju continues]. In Kwangju Citizens' Solidarity, *Panillyun haengwi hwa ch'ŏngsan*. [Inhuman acts and their resolution]. Paper from international symposium; presented May 17, 1995, Kwangju.

———. 2000. "International Law Perspective." In Byun and Lewis, eds.

Pak Yŏng-sun. 1998. "1997 nyŏndo 5.18 Minjung Hangjaeng pusangja 200 myŏng silt'ae pogosŏ" [1997 survey of 200 5.18 People's Uprising injured victims]. Paper presented at 3d annual 5.18 Injured People's Association scholarly meeting, Kwangju, May 16, 1998.

Perry, Elizabeth. 1980. *Rebels and Revolutionaries in North China, 1845–1945*. Stanford: Stanford University Press.

Peterson, Arnold A. 1995. *The 5.18 Kwangju Incident*. Seoul: P'ulpit.

Peterson, Mark. 1988. "Americans and the Kwangju Incident: Problems in the Writing of History." In Clark, ed.

PJC. *See* Catholic Church, Kwangju Diocese Peace and Justice Committee.

Shaw, William, ed. 1991. *Human Rights in Korea: Historical and Political Perspectives*. Cambridge, Mass.: Harvard University Press. Harvard University Studies in East Asian Law, 16.

Shorrock, Tim. 1996. "Ex-Leaders Go on Trial in Seoul." *Journal of Commerce*, February 27, 1996, 1A.

———. 1999. "Kwangju Diary: The View from Washington." In Lee Jae-eui 1999.

Sonn Ho-ch'ŏl. 1995. *Haebang 50 nyŏn ŭi han'guk chŏngch'i* [Korean politics 50 years from liberation]. Seoul: Saegil Press.

Sturken, Marita. 1991. "The Wall, the Screen, and the Image: The Vietnam Veterans Memorial." *Representations* 35 (Summer): 118–142.

Thomas, James Philip. 1993. "Contested from Within and Without: Squatters, the State, the Minjung Movement, and the Limits of Resistance in a

Seoul Shanty Town Targeted for Urban Renewal." Doctoral dissertation, University of Rochester.

USIS (United States Information Service). June 19, 1989. "United States Government Statement on the Events in Kwangju, Republic of Korea, in May 1980." Seoul: United States Embassy Press Office.

Warnberg, Tim. 1988. "The Kwangju Uprising: An Inside View." *Korean Studies* 11: 33–57.

Wells, Kenneth. 1995a. "The Cultural Construction of Korean History." In Wells, ed.

———, ed. 1995b. *South Korea's Minjung Movement: The Culture of Politics and Dissidence*. Honolulu: University of Hawai'i Press.

Yoon Dae-kyu. 1990. *Law and Political Authority in South Korea*. Boulder: Westview Press.

Index

ACC. *See* American Cultural Center

AFKN (American Forces Korea Network), 20, 30, 48

agent provocateurs, 167n8

ajumoni. See Mother

American Cultural Center, 6; attacks on 149, 174n4; friends of, 62; reopening of 174n5

American Embassy. *See* U.S. government

ammaejang. See graves: secret

Anderson, Terry, 47, 165n6

anniversary: celebration of xviii–xix, 32; chairman of, 102, 135–136; events, xix, 99, 169n3; Events Committee for, 135, 155, 158; KCS activities at, 138–141, 142–143; national commemoration of, 103–105, 116–117, 120–122, 160; in 1989, 116; in 1998, 99–105, 120, 130, 139–140, 156, 161–162; in 1995, v, xvii–ix, 116–117, 135–136, 139; in 1997, 120, 121, 130, 140–141, 153, 155 in 1996, 119, 130, 139; tone of, xviii, xix, 108, 152, 155, 157–158; in 2000, ix, 135. *See also* Democratic Drivers' Day; Eve Fest; rituals; Sacred Sites' Pilgrimage

anti-Americanism, 59, 68, 148–149, 157

Asian Human Rights Charter, 139–140, 174n4

Association of Detained (AD), 103, 132, 173n29

autonomy (national), 148, 149

Baker, Donald, 56

Bereaved Families' Association (BFA): for those who died later, 124–125; government oppression of 113–115; history of, 112–113, 172n16; political activism by, 114–116; political displacement of 120–122

"Black Beret" special forces. *See* paratroopers

brutality. *See* paratroopers: brutality of; violence; massacres

censorship (government): 168n2; during 5.18, 4–5; of Kwangju during Fifth Republic, 60, 75–76, 93, 165n3, 172n8

ch'aryang siwi. See vehicle demonstrations

Cheju Uprising, 119, 173n17

chesa, 117, 119, 123. *See also* rituals

chinsang kyumyŏng. See Finding the Truth

Cho A-ra, 28, 64, 146

Cho Kyŏng-suk. *See* Mother

Ch'oe Mi-ae, 23

Choi Kyu-ha, 5, 39, 45, 59

Chŏlla region: anti-government sentiment in, vii, 109; discrimination against xvi–xvii, 5, 13, 91–92; and 5.18, 30, 61. *See also* regionalism

chonyaje. See Eve Fest

Chun Doo Hwan: effigy of, 41; and 5.18, 39; repression of free speech, 76;

185

About the Author

LINDA S. LEWIS, WHO IS associate professor of anthropology and director of the East Asian Studies Program at Wittenberg University,
received her doctorate in cultural anthropology from Columbia University. She first went to Korea in 1970 as a Peace Corps Volunteer and
later did her doctoral dissertation research in the district court in
Kwangju in 1979–1980. As an eyewitness to the events of May 18, she
has had a longstanding personal and scholarly interest in the Kwangju
Uprising.